SHORTER ATLAS
OF THE CLASSICAL WORLD

SHORTER ATLAS
OF THE
CLASSICAL WORLD

H. H. SCULLARD, F.B.A., F.S.A.

Professor of Ancient History, King's College,
University of London

and

A. A. M. VAN DER HEYDEN, Hist. Drs.

1962

THOMAS NELSON AND SONS LTD

Parkside Works Edinburgh 9
36 Park Street London W1
117 Latrobe Street Melbourne C1

302–304 Barclays Bank Building
Commissioner and Kruis Streets
Johannesburg

THOMAS NELSON AND SONS (CANADA) LTD
91–93 Wellington Street West Toronto 1

THOMAS NELSON AND SONS
18 East 41st Street New York 17, N.Y.

SOCIÉTÉ FRANÇAISE D'ÉDITIONS NELSON
97 rue Monge Paris 5

CONTENTS

GREECE   *page*

    Map 1.   Greece (front endpaper)
The Geographical Setting   9
Minoan and Mycenean Civilisation   13
The Rise of the City-States   26
    Map 2.   Greece in the Period 1000–800 B.C.
    Map 3.   Greek Settlements around Mediterranean and Black Sea
Early Greek Civilisation   42
Greece and Persia   54
    Map 4.   Persian Wars: Darius
    Map 5.   Persian Wars: Xerxes
The Age of Pericles   69
    Map 6.   Athens at the Zenith of its Power
Athens and Sparta   83
The Rise of Macedon and Alexander the Great   87
    Map 7.   Alexander the Great
    Map 8.   The Hellenistic Kingdoms ca. 280 B.C.
The Hellenistic World   100

ROME

    Map 14. Italy (back endpaper)
Early Italy   113
    Map 9.   Early Italy
Early Rome   115
Rome and the Mediterranean World (264–133 B.C.)   130
    Map 10. The Second Punic War
Early Roman Life and Culture   136
    Map 11. Campaigns of Gaius Julius Caesar
The Fall of the Republic   149
Life in the Days of Cicero   165
    Map 12. The Roman Empire in the Time of Augustus
The Augustan Age   167
The Early Empire (to A.D. 193)   181
Life under the Empire   196
    Map 13. The Roman Empire in the Second Century A.D.
The Later Empire   210
Epilogue   215
Notes to the plates   226
Index   230

*Maps 2–8 are between pages 28 and 29, and Maps 9–13 are between
pages 116 and 117*

INTRODUCTION

The series of Atlases published by Messrs. Thomas Nelson will have familiarised their readers with the extended use of the word Atlas to include not merely a collection of maps, but also of illustrations and explanatory text. This further contribution to the series therefore comprises maps and a brief sketch of the history and achievements of the Greeks and Romans, together with illustrations that are designed to make more vivid some aspects of the geography of the classical world and to give a few glimpses of its cultural glories.

It should be made quite clear that this is not an abridged version of the *Atlas of the Classical World*, of which the English edition was published in 1959; it is essentially a new work although planned on the same general lines. Fresh maps have been drawn, the great majority of the illustrations are new and a completely new text has been written by myself. The needs of schools and of the general reader have been kept in mind.

The smaller format has necessitated simpler maps, containing only the more important place names, in contrast to the fuller and more elaborate maps and plans of the larger work. The text is designed to sketch the general development of classical history, with special reference to its geographical background, together with a brief appreciation of the cultural achievements of the Greeks and Romans. It is to be hoped that the illustrations any stimulate the imagination where considerations of space preclude lengthy descriptions: thus, to take but one example, it will not escape the reader's notice that the photographs of the Acropolis of Athens (nos. 9 and 10) have been chosen to illustrate what is said on page 11 about the growth of the city-state with its rocky citadel and cluster of houses below.

Severe compression and selection have been necessary in order to produce this book at the modest price for which it sells. This, in so far as the Atlas may be used in schools, can be balanced by the teacher's fuller explanations, but at the same time it is hoped that the general reader will gain a true, if necessarily limited, impression of the achievements of Greek and Roman civilisation and of the geographical setting in which these two peoples lived out their lives. Classical history and culture can never be understood without a firm grasp of the physical conditions of the Mediterranean basin, while the study of geography tends to be somewhat arid until it is related to the reaction of man to his physical environment.

It is a commonplace, but nevertheless true, that much that is best in modern Western civilisation is rooted and grounded in the world of Greece and Rome. The third great force that has helped to mould it, Christianity, although its early history belongs to the Graeco-Roman world, has been excluded from this volume, since its early growth has been treated more fully in separate volumes, the *Atlas of the Bible*, the *Shorter Atlas of the Bible* and the *Atlas of the Early Christian World*.

King's College, London. May. 1962. H. H. SCULLARD

THE GEOGRAPHICAL SETTING

Ancient civilisations developed where they did largely because of geographical and climatic factors. Not that man has not shaped his own history; but the manner in which he has done this has been **strongly** influenced by his natural setting. The growth of Egyptian civilisation was made possible only by the life-giving waters of the Nile, while the cultural achievements of the Sumerians, Babylonians, Assyrians, and other peoples in Mesopotamian lands rested upon a physical environment conditioned by the rivers Euphrates and Tigris. The unifying factor in the classical world of Greece and Rome was the Mediterranean Sea. We may tend now to think of the countries around this great inland sea as separate and unconnected: they belong to the three different continents of Europe, Asia, and Africa. But in classical times men learned to think of them as parts of a common world. This came about not only because they were cut off from the great land-masses behind them by mountains or deserts, and thus tended to look inwards towards their common sea, but also because they shared a similar climate and geological structure. Despite local variations, this climate is so distinctive that modern geographers have adopted the 'Mediterranean climate' as a type which they can apply to similar climates found in corresponding situations in such different parts of the world as America and Australia.

Climatic conditions in the Mediterranean world in ancient times probably differed little from those prevailing today. Though not everywhere so attractive as those of a few favoured spots such as the French Riviera, these conditions are in general less severe than those in northern European countries. In winter long periods of continuous cold are rare, and although rainfall is heavy and often accompanied by squalls, the skies quickly clear. The summers are sunny and hot, but the heat is dry and less taxing than a humid heat. The mean July temperature in London is 62°, in Rome 76°, and in Athens 80°, while those of January are 38°, 45°, and 48° respectively; some districts, in Sicily or southern Spain, are even milder in winter and hotter in summer. In winter squally storms tend to turn the smaller rivers into raging torrents and to wash away the relatively light soil in those mountainous districts that are not well forested, while the summer may produce prolonged droughts and convert the riverbeds into dry tracks. Nevertheless the winter tends to invigorate men after the heat of summer, and the unusual clarity and freshness of the air stimulates both body and mind.

Similar climatic conditions naturally produce a fairly uniform type of vegetation. This is rich and luxuriant in the lowlands where there is a good supply of water, but much of the higher ground produces little but bush and scrub – and a large part of both Greece and Italy is mountainous. Most Mediterranean lands therefore produced the same kind of crops, and similar methods of working the land were devised. The chief products were cereal plants, vines, and olives. Olive oil was used not only for human consumption, but also for lighting and washing purposes. Though cattle and horses were reared, the chief grazing animals were sheep and goats, which could provide material for clothing as well as milk. The need for varied pasture, highlands in summer and lowlands in winter, led to seasonal movements of flocks and shepherds, the 'transhumance' which is still practised in Greece and Italy.

These general conditions not only affected economic life but had their repercussions on social and even political development. The genial climate encouraged open-air life. Much more time was spent out of doors than in northern countries. Men met their friends for pleasure or business in the open. Thus in the central squares of cities colonnades and porticos would be provided to give temporary shelter from sun or rain. Entertainment also was enjoyed in unroofed theatres and arenas, and even official business might be transacted under the sky: in Athens the popular assemblies and courts met in the open, and at Rome magistrates dispensed justice in the Forum. Private houses of any size were built around a small open courtyard. The houses of the gods, temples, were generally small, and large gatherings of worshippers would congregate at open shrines outside. All this naturally stimulated free social intercourse and communal life.

The two great mountainous peninsulas of Greece and Italy, thrusting southwards into the Mediterranean, are separated only by the Adriatic Sea, but in fact they tend to face away from one another and to lie back to back. This is due partly to the relative lack of good harbours on the east coast of Italy and on the west coast of the Balkans. The natural direction for Greek expansion is towards Asia Minor across the Aegean Sea, where the way is made easy by the great number of islands *en route*. Similarly the contacts of Italy tended to be with the lands of the western Mediterranean. As the distance from Sicily, at Italy's toe, to north Africa is less than one hundred miles, Italy tends to divide the whole Mediterranean into two parts. First the Carthaginians and then the Romans tried to turn the western half into a private preserve, *mare nostrum;* Carthage finally had to abandon the attempt, but Rome succeeded and then extended its influence over the eastern half as well. But the subsequent Roman Empire, although a closely-knit political unit, always comprised two parts, a Greek East and a Latin West; and it was the latter, namely Italy and the Romanised lands of Gaul, Spain, and North Africa, that formed the solid base and core of the Empire.

Two natural features that profoundly influenced man's development in Greece were the mountains and the sea. Although the main direction of the mountain ranges is from north to south, subsequent partial collapses resulted in fractures which cut across the chief ranges and created a tangled confusion of mountain and plain, with arms of the sea often intruding. One result is that only some 20 per cent of the land surface is level and even less is cultivable. Communications between these resultant pockets of land are generally difficult and arduous. Thus village and town life tended to develop in semi-isolated self-contained cantons, comprising an area of cultivable plain frequently with some mountainous ground (which would provide summer pasture) and access to the sea. Indeed communications were often easier by sea than by land, and the separate Greek communities were too independent to create a proper network of roads. In parts of the country little advance was made beyond village life, which continued as late as the fourth century B.C. In those districts where larger collections of men congregated into towns, the settlement would normally be situated on defensible high ground above a pocket of fertile land, chosen partly with regard to the water supply. The citadel (or acropolis) was the *polis* proper, while the houses below were called the *astu* (this is well illustrated by the growth of Athens or Corinth). Good building stone was plentiful, and the mineral wealth of Greece included rich veins of marble, excellent potter's clay, and scattered mines of copper (in Euboea), silver (at Laurium in Attica), and gold (at Thasos and Mt. Pangaeus in Thrace).

The sea was never far from most of the Greeks: nowhere in the Peloponnese is it more than 32 miles distant, and at no point in central Greece is it farther than 40 miles away, while the indented coastline of 2,600 miles is nearly 500 miles longer than that of Italy, although the land surface is only one-third the area of Italy. Further, in summer the sea tempers the climate of the mainland: trade winds sweep across the Aegean, and breezes spring up from the sea in the afternoons, to be followed after dark by land breezes which help to keep the air circulating. Although sailing was virtually suspended during the winter months, and in some areas was hazardous even in summer, yet navigation was greatly assisted by the mountains: not only was the Aegean full of islands, which are the protruding peaks of a drowned plateau, but the mainland also provided many landmarks that were visible afar. The sea also made a further contribution to economic life, besides providing a means of communication for the development of overseas trade: it produced food, in particular the tunny fish. Thus while the mountains in the north helped to keep the land free from invaders and to turn its face southwards, the sea provided a means of expansion throughout the whole Mediterranean area.

Italy also was dominated by mountain and sea. Few parts are more than 70 miles from the coast. Its northern borders are protected by the barrier of the Alps. The great plain in the north between the Alps and the Apennines was long considered to be part of Gaul (Cisalpine Gaul); it was incorporated in the administrative system of Italy only at the end of the Roman Republic. Thence southwards the Apennines run the length of the peninsula, reaching in places nearly 10,000 feet (the height of Mount Olympus in Greece). They approach closer to the eastern than to the western coast and leave little room for any fertile land in the east until the moorlands of Apulia are reached; nor does the east coast provide good harbours. Thus the main development was on the west of the central chain. South of the irregular hills of Etruria, which is marked off by the Arno and Tiber, the central highlands approach the western coast in the Volscian hills, to the north and south of which they leave room for the two plains of Latium and Campania. Into these fertile plains, which were enriched by volcanic ash, the highlanders constantly tried to press in early days. Despite the long coastline of Italy, the interests of a large part of the early population long remained agricultural and continental rather than maritime, although early settlers had landed from the sea (Greeks in the south, and Etruscans, attracted by the mines, in the north). This was partly because the Greeks had occupied the best harbours (such as Tarentum and those on the Bay of Naples) and also because there were few harbours or navigable rivers farther up the west coast. The Romans and Latins were essentially farmers and peasants. But once Italy had been united under Rome's leadership, a process facilitated by Roman roadbuilders, the importance of its central position within the Mediterranean was realised both by Rome itself and by the other Mediterranean powers.

MINOAN AND MYCENAEAN
CIVILISATION

The Greeks told how the Athenian hero Theseus sailed to Cnossus in the island of Crete and there slew the monstrous Minotaur, half bull, half man, who in the labyrinthine palace of the king destroyed the young men and girls that Athens was compelled to send every seven years as tribute. Whether the Greeks of the fifth century B.C. thought of this story as history or legend, they certainly knew almost nothing about the real historical background from which it sprang. Nor indeed was modern man much better informed until some sixty years ago, when the excavations conducted by Sir Arthur Evans in Crete revealed the existence of a virtually unknown civilisation and thereby startled the contemporary world, which knew much about the early empires in Egypt and Mesopotamia but had not expected to see another civilisation uncovered that was worthy to be compared with those already known.

This early culture, which has been called Minoan after Minos the legendary ruler of Cnossus, flourished with its centre in Crete during the Bronze Age from before the middle of the third millennium B.C. for more than a thousand years. The origin of the people who developed it is uncertain; they probably came from southwest Asia Minor, perhaps with some admixture of Libyans from the south, but they most probably did not speak an Indo-European language and were therefore not of the same stock as the later Greeks. They exploited the natural wealth of Crete, cultivating corn, vines, and olives (the basis of life of most of the peoples of the Mediterranean world); they domesticated sheep, goats, and oxen, and they showed great skill in the production of pottery and metal-work. Thus they developed an increasingly civilised manner of life, which was centred on the royal palaces, particularly those of Cnossus and Phaestus. As their numbers, strength, and wealth increased, they became, especially after about 1700 B.C., a world power. One reason for this was the geographical position of the island, which commands a central position in the eastern Mediterranean. Their natural abilities included great skill in seafaring and navigation, so that before long their merchant ships were faring far and wide. It was no great distance to Egypt (where Cretans are represented in a painting of the fifteenth century), the islands of the Aegean, Greece, Asia Minor, Cyprus, or Syria. Thus the Minoans were able to build up a widespread commerce and thereby acquired great wealth. This allowed them to develop a rich and luxurious civilisation.

Many aspects of this have been revealed by archaeology, particularly by the uncovering of the great palace at Cnossus, which spread over some five acres and contained so many rooms and passages that it gave rise to the story of the Labyrinth. The paintings on its walls depict many aspects of Cretan life, including the physical appearance of the men and women, their dress and jewellery and their bull-baiting sports. Life, at any rate in court circles, appears refined and elegant, and the artistic inspiration of their pottery and metal-work shows considerable *joie de vivre*. Their religion was based on nature worship, particularly of a Mother Goddess, with the double-axe as a cult symbol. Animal-headed demons, which appear later, suggest a darker side to their beliefs.

Of their literature, if it existed, nothing has survived, but we have evidence of their writing. At first they used a pictorial script, but after about 1800 B.C. this was replaced by a syllabic script which has been called Linear A. As this has not been deciphered, the language it records remains unknown. In the palace there have survived numerous clay tablets which clearly record lists of goods, no doubt stores and tribute. Thus the palace was evidently not only the residence of the king and his court but formed the administrative centre of a highly-organised bureaucratic state and empire. On the whole life appears to have been peaceful, since the palaces were unfortified and body-armour is not found until a late period. But in the fifteenth century B.C. a great change took place, and to understand this we must now turn to the mainland of Greece.

In the third millennium B.C. a population not dissimilar from the early inhabitants of Crete entered Greece, perhaps by sea from the southeast, but soon after 2000 B.C. Greece was invaded, probably from the north, by Indo-European tribes, whom the later Greeks called Achaeans. They made pottery on the wheel and built houses with a large hall and central hearth, the so-called *megaron* type. From 1700 or 1600 B.C. they were subjected to strong cultural influences from Crete, so that in many respects the external appearance of their way of life began to resemble the Minoan. This interplay of Cretan on Helladic culture (so archaeologists have named Greek mainland culture in the Bronze Age) resulted in Mycenaean civilisation, so called from its centre at Mycenae, where a dynasty of strong kings built up the power and wealth of the city that Homer justly called 'rich in gold'. These royal personages were buried in the shaft-graves discovered by Schliemann in 1876 and also later in domed tombs called *tholoi* or 'beehive tombs', such as the one that has been misnamed the Treasury of Atreus.

	A AI	E	I	O	U
(H-)	A / AI	E	I	O	U
D-	DA	DE	DI	DO	DU
JA-	JA	JE		JO	
K-G-CH-	KA	KE / KWE?	KI	KO	KU
M-	MA	ME	MI	MO	
N-	NA / NWA?	NE / NEKO?	NI	NO	NU
B-P-PH-	PA	PE / PTE	PI	PO	PU
QU-GU-		QE	QI?	QO	
R-L-	RA / RJA	RE	RI	RO / RJO	RU
S-	SA	SE	SI	SO	SU
T-TH-	TA / TJA?	TE	TI	TO	TU
W-	WA	WE	WI	WO	
Z-		ZE		ZO	ZU?

Mycenaean syllabary: Linear B with suggested phonetic values.

Mycenae, with its royal palace on a fortified citadel, surrounded by 'cyclopaean' walls in which was the famous Lion Gate, soon became the dominant power in the Peloponnese, although there were other powerful states like Tiryns and Nestor's kingdom at Pylos. 'Mycenaean' settlements are also found at Athens, in Boeotia in central Greece, and in southern Thessaly at Iolcos, and a large part of Greece was embraced by a uniform culture.

The influence of these Mycenaeans spread far afield; like the Minoans, they traded widely, and their exported pottery is found as far west as Sicily and southern Italy (Lipari Islands), in Egypt, Rhodes, Cyprus, northern Syria, and on the coast of Asia Minor at Miletus. In some of these places their influence is so strong as to suggest actual settlements. But they could not penetrate far into Asia Minor, since this was dominated by the empire of the Hittites, with whom they may have had diplomatic contacts.

During the second half of the fifteenth century they raided Crete and succeeded in occupying Cnossus. This has been demonstrated by the recent decipherment of the Linear B tablets which are found both at Cnossus and widely in Greece (e.g. at Pylos and Mycenae). It is clear that when they seized Cnossus the Mycenaeans took over not merely the administration of the palace and of the towns that Cnossus had ruled but also the syllabic script which they adapted in order to write their own language (Linear B). Now that it has been shown that the language of these tablets was an early form of Greek it is clear that the Mycenaean civilisation in Greece was essentially Greek. How long these Mycenaean Greeks held Cnossus is uncertain, but it has generally been supposed that Cnossus was destroyed about 1400 B.C. The palace was sacked, and the widespread destruction is less likely to be due to a great raid by sea from the eastern Mediterranean than to an uprising of the native population against its overlords. Whatever the cause, Minoan civilisation, according to the general view, soon withered and died.

But the Mycenaeans in Greece continued to flourish for some time, and thanks to the evidence of the tablets we now know much more about their political, economic, and social life. Their states were monarchies with apparently a feudal system of barons and a highly centralised palace bureaucracy (such as had existed at Cnossus). The tablets, which are

The geographical setting. High mountain ranges with peaks rising almost to the snowline interlace the whole of Greece. 1. Mt. Helicon in Boeotia, the 'abode of the Muses' (5,150 ft.). 2. Rivers are of little importance, being too turbulent in winter and too shallow in summer. 3. In antiquity as now, olives played an important economic rôle: the plain of Marathon, clad in thousands of olive-trees. 4. The Alpheus, narrow at first, progressively widening, meanders through Arcadia, a district in the Peloponnese. Higher regions, like the uplands round the temple at Bassae (5), usually bear no vegetation except brushwood. 6, 7. Mountains and sea greatly influenced the development of the Greeks. The mountain ranges that divide the country promoted the rise of independent states, while the sea, dotted with islands and often calm, made possible the brilliant expansion of the Greeks.

3

4

6

7

9

10

concerned with administration and stores, reveal something of the system of land tenure and of the varied occupations of the labourers and slaves. Many of the deities who were worshipped by the later Greeks, such as Zeus, Hera, Poseidon, and Athene, were known to the Mycenaeans.

It was these Greeks who fought the Trojan War immortalised in Homer's *Iliad*. However much the story has been elaborated, a historical event certainly lies behind it, and men like Agamemnon and Achilles led an expedition which overthrew Troy. This city on the Dardanelles had already enjoyed a long existence: the sixth city (i.e. the sixth from the bottom of the superimposed settlements that archaeologists have revealed) had flourished for several centuries until destroyed by earthquake about 1300 B.C. Thereafter it had been rebuilt, and it was this city (VIIA) that the Greeks destroyed (traditionally in 1183 B.C.; some would date it about fifty years earlier). Troy fell at a time of considerable unrest in the eastern Mediterranean following upon the collapse of the Minoan and Hittite empires. Bands of men roved the seas, raiding where they could: two such invasions of the 'Peoples of the Seas' were beaten off by the Egyptians, in 1221 and 1194. In these unsettled times Greek trade with the East was disrupted, and many of their overseas settlements were lost. Soon the home country itself was affected, already weakened perhaps by its great effort against Troy. However that may be, the Mycenaeans were unable successfully to withstand a wave of invasions by Dorian Greeks who poured southwards from northwest Greece and destroyed most of the great cities like Mycenae and Pylos. A period of history was ending. The degree of unity that Greece had enjoyed between 1400 and 1200 was gone, and the great days of Crete and Mycenae were soon almost forgotten amid the confusion of unsettled times, surviving only, transmuted and distorted, in the folk memory of poem and myth as a heroic golden age.

The geographical setting. 8. For most Greeks the sea was not far off: numerous inlets along the coastline penetrate deep into the land. 9. The cities usually arose round ⟨ defensible height, which later developed from a fortress into a city centre. The Athenian Acropolis, rising high above the surrounding plain, is a good example of this outstanding feature of many Greek cities. The buildings that now cluster at the foot of the Acropolis (10) recall the ancient city, or *astu*, which was built against the slope of the Acropolis. 11. View of the Athenian Acropolis from the Southwest showing the Parthenon, the finest Doric temple of Athens, built in the 5the century B.C[8] 12. In the course of their expansion overseas the Greeks established a second homeland in southern Italy, where fertile plains offered sites for the many new cities they built.

25

THE RISE OF THE CITY-STATES

During the period in which the Dorians gradually overran Greece, many new features appeared in various parts of the country: the use of the Doric dialect, of iron, of cremation in place of burial, pottery decorated with geometric patterns. On the other hand, the use of writing and the art of building in stone were lost. As the various peoples were thrust around, many (including some of the invading Dorians themselves) found that Greece was too small to support them all, and various waves of emigrants sought new homes across the Aegean on the coast of Asia Minor and the off-shore islands. Aeolians settled in the northern part (e.g. at Smyrna, Cyme, Lesbos), Ionians from Attica in the central area (e.g. at Miletus and Chios), and Dorians from the Peloponnese in the south (e.g. Cnidus, Rhodes, Cos). Greeks who arrived in Cyprus clashed with the Phoenician merchants, who were building up trade links throughout the Mediterranean. But if economic and political rivalry between Greek and Phoenician grew sharp, the Greeks gained one inestimable gift from the Phoenicians: the alphabet. They took over the Phoenician alphabet (roughly that of the Hebrew of the Old Testament) and adapted it to their own use, thereby devising a much more flexible instrument than the forgotten syllabic writing of their Mycenaean predecessors.

The Greek settlements in Asia Minor quickly prospered, thanks partly to the relative fertility of the land. They developed city life, first under kings and then under oligarchies, and many of their cities became rich from trade with the Aegean, Euxine (Black Sea), and the interior of Asia Minor. As these Asiatic Greeks recalled memories of the heroic days of Mycenae, a body of epic poetry developed which flowered into the *Iliad* and *Odyssey*. It was probably in the eighth century B.C. that these poems received their present form in all essentials. The author was Homer, who lived in Chios – at least so it was believed as early as the sixth century.

Meanwhile in Greece itself, though many people continued to live in tribes and villages, others began to collect into centres and to develop city life. Thus the great cities of classical Greece, including Sparta, Athens, Thebes, Corinth, and others, began to emerge. But soon all were faced with a crucial problem: as Herodotus said, Greece and Poverty were foster-sisters, and the land simply was not fertile enough to support a population which began to increase rapidly with the return of more settled times. All the cities needed more land, and while Athens tried to ignore the problem and Sparta solved it by seizing land from its neighbours, most cities responded to the difficulty by sending groups of their citizens to seek new homes elsewhere. These colonies, when established, became independent states, bound to their mother-cities only by ties of sentiment. Additional motives stimulated the movement: political oppression by the ruling class at home or the attractions of trade supplemented the spur of land hunger. Colonisation developed into an epoch-making movement, which between 750 and 600 B.C. changed the whole face of the Mediterranean world and spread Greek civilisation far and wide. Colonies were established around the shores of the Euxine, the Propontis (Sea of Marmora), the northern Aegean (e.g. Chalcidice), in Sicily and round the heel and toe of Italy as far north as Cumae (the colonies in this last area were so numerous that it was later known as Magna Graecia), in southern France (Massilia, which in turn sent a few colonies to Spain), in Cyrene, and even one colony (Naucratis) in Egypt. This sudden outburst was not paralleled again in world history until the colonisation from Europe in the sixteenth century onwards. And not only did it extend the area of Greek civilisation, but it also helped to develop the natural gifts of the Greeks, their courage, sense of adventure, and self-reliance, while at the same time they began to contrast themselves with the 'barbarians' on the fringes of their areas of settlement. These natives were not looked down on because they might happen to belong to a different racial stock from the Greeks (the ancient world was singularly free from racial prejudices) but because they lacked the culture which the Greeks began to recognise as a common bond among themselves.

In the north of Greece lay the large fertile plain of Thessaly, where the invading Greeks had reduced the early population to serfs (called *penestae*) and ruled the land as feudal barons. Thessaly became very strong in the seventh century and even dominated a small League of Neighbours (Amphictyonic League) established around Thermopylae; but its power soon declined, partly because it was surrounded by mountains and was largely self-sufficient, somewhat cut off from the rest of Greece. To the south lay Boeotia, which was essentially an agricultural country; by the sixth century its small cities had managed to unite into a League, but these early federal movements were not strong enough to overcome the intense love of complete independence which animated most Greeks. Indeed one of the greatest weaknesses of the Greeks was their unwillingness to limit in any way the sovereignty of their individual city-states, even when federal unions might have helped them to stem external pressure or danger. In Phocis, the neighbour of Boeotia, was the independent city of Delphi, famed for its temple and oracle of Apollo, which was consulted by Greeks from near and far. Many competitors also came to contend in the Games of Pythian Apollo, so that Delphi became an important pan-Hellenic centre and its priests exercised both a unifying and humanising influence upon Greek life. Just off the east coast lay the long, mountainous island of Euboea, whose two chief cities, Eretria and Chalcis, prospered early and became trade rivals; they both took a large part in the colonising movement, in the northern Aegean (in Chalcidice) and in Italy and Sicily in the west. In the Peloponnese the first city to become powerful was Argos, near the almost forgotten Mycenae. Under its king Pheidon early in the seventh century it clashed with Sparta, Corinth, and Athens, and tried to gain control of Olympia, where a four-yearly festival of Zeus had started in 776 B.C. and soon attracted competitors from all Greece. But the power of Argos was short-lived. Another great city in the Peloponnese was the isthmus town of Corinth, which built up its trade, especially with the West. Its early pottery (proto-Corinthian) and its bronze-work were much in demand, and its trade-routes to the west were strengthened by the founding of colonies at Corcyra and Syracuse (unlike other Greek cities, Corinth tried to retain some control over its colonies). By 700 B.C. Corinth was the leading sea-power in Greece.

The leadership of the Peloponnese, however, fell to Sparta. The Dorian invaders here reduced the population to serfs (*Helots*) or semi-serfs (*Perioekoi*). With the Helots to work the land for them, the conquerors formed the state, a small exclusive body of some 4,000 men. But soon the population grew too numerous for the Eurotas valley to support, and the Spartans looked for fresh land. In two long wars in the eighth and seventh centuries they conquered the neighbouring Messenians, who were forced to become Helots and work the land for their new masters. The cultural life of early Sparta was similar to that of other Greek cities, until it suddenly militarised the state, partly because of the needs of the second Messenian War, partly from fear of revolt by the Helots, and partly from fear of its rival Argos. Thus about 600 B.C. the military organisation was changed, and a rigid social structure was imposed on all the citizens, under which they were trained from the cradle to the grave to serve the

Map 2:

GREECE IN THE PERIOD
1000 — 800 B.C.
THE EARLY MIGRATIONS

Ionians
Aeolians
Northwest Greeks, related to the Dorians
Arcadians
Dorians
Main centres of political and religious life

Smyrna: Aeolian settlement, overrun at an early date by the Ionians.

Ionian possessions in the Aegean and in Asia Minor were more important than those in Greece itself.

Dodona, Larisa, Peneus, THESSALIA, EPIRUS, Leucas, ACARNANIA, Achelous, AETOLIA, LOCRIS, PHOCIS, Delphi, BOEOTIA, Thebae, Cephallenia, ACHAIA, Megara, ATTICA, acynthos, ELIS, ARCADIA, Corinthus, Athenae, Olympia, Mycenae, Salamis, Argos, Aegina, MESSENIA, Sparta, LACONIA, Cythera

Imbros, Lemnos, Troia, PHRYGIA, Assus, MYSIA, Mitylene, Lesbos, Scyros, Cyme, Phocaea, Hermus, Clazomenae, Smyrna, LYDIA, Chios, Erythrae, Colophon, Ephesus, Andros, Samos, Priene, Icaros, Miletus, Didyma, CARIA, Paros, Naxos, Halicarnassus, Cos, Cnidus, Melos, Ialysus, Thera, Camirus, Rhodos, Lindus, Cythera, Carpathos, Euboea

Cnossus

C r e t a

2

Map 3:

GREEK SETTLEMENTS AROUND
THE MEDITERRANEAN
AND THE BLACK SEA
8th — 6th centuries B.C.

Area of Greek colonisation
Area from which colonies were founded

e.g. Tanais, e.g. Tyras Olbia, Panticapeum, e.g. Massilia Nicaea, e.g. Emporiae, e.g. Olynthus Byzantium Odessus Istrus, e.g. Epidamnus, e.g. Chalcedon Sinope Trapezus, Hemeroscopeum, Cumae, Maenace, e.g. Taras Croton Syracusae Acragas, e.g. Cyrene Barca, Naucratis

3

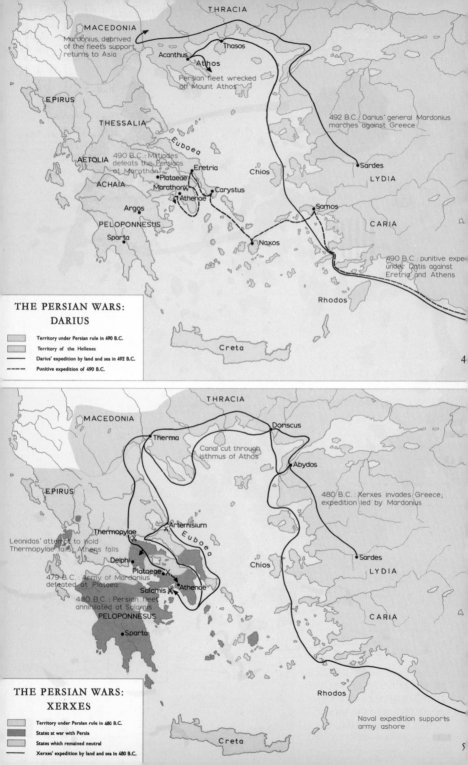

THRACIA

MACEDONIA
Mardonius, deprived
of the fleet's support,
returns to Asia

Acanthus● ●Thasos

Athos

Persian fleet wrecked
off Mount Athos

492 B.C.: Darius' general Mardonius
marches against Greece

EPIRUS

THESSALIA

Euboea

AETOLIA 490 B.C.: Miltiades
defeats the Persians
at Marathon

ACHAIA

●Plataeae
Marathon✗
●Athenae

Eretria●
Carystus●

Chios

●Sardes

LYDIA

Argos●

PELOPONNESUS

Sparta●

Naxos●

●Samos

CARIA

490 B.C.: punitive expe
under Datis against
Eretria and Athens

Rhodos

Creta

THE PERSIAN WARS:
DARIUS

Territory under Persian rule in 490 B.C.

Territory of the Hellenes

Darius' expedition by land and sea in 492 B.C.

Punitive expedition of 490 B.C.

4

THRACIA

MACEDONIA

●Therma

Doriscus●

Canal cut through
isthmus of Athos

●Abydos

480 B.C.: Xerxes invades Greece;
expedition led by Mardonius

EPIRUS

Artemisium
✗
Thermopylae
✗

Euboea

Leonidas' attempt to hold
Thermopylae fails; Athens falls

Delphi●

Chios

●Sardes

LYDIA

479 B.C.: Army of Mardonius
defeated at Plataea

Plataeae ✗

Salamis✗
●Athenae

480 B.C.: Persian fleet
annihilated at Salamis

PELOPONNESUS

CARIA

Sparta●

Rhodos

THE PERSIAN WARS:
XERXES

Territory under Persian rule in 480 B.C.

States at war with Persia

States which remained neutral

Xerxes' expedition by land and sea in 480 B.C.

Naval expedition supports
army ashore

Creta

5

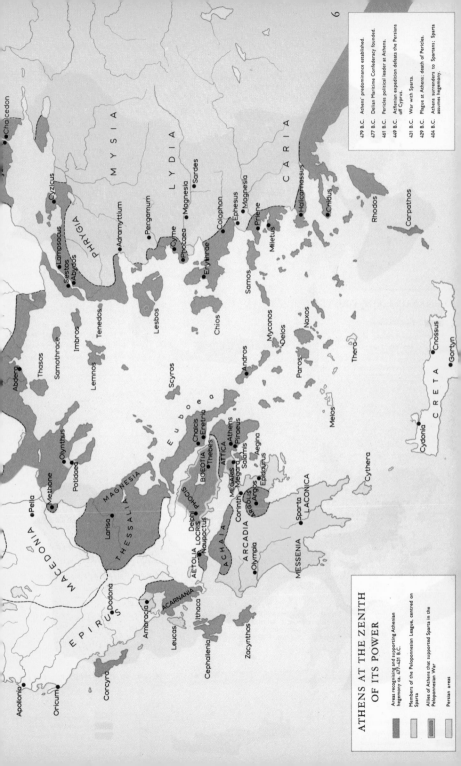

6

ATHENS AT THE ZENITH OF ITS POWER

479 B.C.   Athens' predominance established.

477 B.C.   Delian Maritime Confederacy founded.

461 B.C.   Pericles political leader at Athens.

449 B.C.   Athenian expedition defeats the Persians off Cyprus.

431 B.C.   War with Sparta.

429 B.C.   Plague at Athens; death of Pericles.

404 B.C.   Athens surrenders to Spartans; Sparta assumes hegemony.

Areas recognizing and supporting Athenian hegemony ca. 477–431 B.C.

Members of the Peloponnesian League, centred on Sparta

Allies of Athens that supported Sparta in the Peloponnesian War

Persian areas

CHALCEDON

MYSIA

LYDIA

CARIA

Cyzicus

Lampsacus

Sestos

Abydos

PHRYGIA

Adramyttium

Pergamum

Sardes

Magnesia

Cyme

Phocaea

Erythrae

Colophon

Ephesus

Magnesia

Priene

Miletus

Halicarnassus

Cnidus

Rhodos

Carpathos

Samos

Chios

Lesbos

Tenedos

Lemnos

Imbros

Samothrace

Thasos

Abdera

Myconos

Delos

Naxos

Paros

Thera

Andros

Scyros

Euboea

Melos

CRETA

Cnossus

Gortyn

Cydonia

Cythera

Chalcis

Eretria

BOEOTIA

Thebes

ATTICA

Athens

Piraeus

Salamis

Aegina

MEGARIS

Megara

Corinth

Epidaurus

ARGOLIS

Argos

Sparta

LACONICA

MESSENIA

Olympia

ARCADIA

ACHAIA

AETOLIA

LOCRIS

Naupactus

Delphi

PHOCIS

MAGNESIA

THESSALIA

Larisa

Methone

Pella

Potidaea

Olynthus

MACEDONIA

EPIRUS

Dodona

ACARNANIA

Ambracia

Leucas

Ithaca

Cephallenia

Zacynthos

Corcyra

Oricum

Apollonia

state in a hide-bound military system. Sparta turned in upon itself, renounced trade and foreign contacts, and set out to breed and train soldiers. The constitution also was somewhat unusual. Sparta retained monarchy when other cities were renouncing it; in fact there were two kings, who were advised by a body of twenty-eight nobles (the *Gerousia*). The people, although meeting in an Assembly (the *Apella*), had little influence until five magistrates called ephors began to represent their interests and to check kings and Council. But even Sparta found that conquest might not be the best of activities. After a long struggle against Arcadia, the mountainous centre of the Peloponnese, it failed to reduce Tegea and so turned to the idea of alliance in place of conquest. Tegea was made an ally (ca. 550) and before long most of the Peloponnesians had been brought into alliance (the so-called Peloponnesian League), although Argos remained a perennial enemy.

Meantime great political, economic, and social changes were taking place in most of the cities of Greece. Monarchy had declined; the royal houses sank to the level of other noble houses, who vied with each other for preeminence in the administration of their cities in the spheres of justice, religion, and war. These aristocracies based their claim to rule on birth and the possession of land; they maintained their power partly through their cavalry. But economic conditions were changing, partly as a result of the introduction of coined money, a most useful device that the Greeks gradually borrowed from Lydia in the course of the seventh century. This stimulated and facilitated trade and industry, with the result that in many cities men outside the narrow circle of nobles were growing rich and demanding political influence. Further, the wars were being fought very largely by the middle-class yeomen, men who could provide themselves with full personal armour and who as 'hoplite' infantry now formed the backbone of the battle-line. Thus the older aristocracies were often forced to open their ranks to the wealthy commercial classes, and political power, although still wielded by only a few (oligarchy), now derived from wealth of all kinds and not merely from land; thus the state became a 'timocracy'.

But pressure from the middle classes, who knew their value to the state in war, and from the lower classes, many of whom were in distressing economic need, led to the demand for reform. In many cities men cried out for the publication of the hitherto unwritten laws, for greater social justice, and for more political influence. In some cases the need was met by appointing a lawgiver (e.g. Solon at Athens, as will be seen below), but a more drastic solution was found in those cities where a single person seized power unconstitutionally. Such a 'tyrant' (a word that long remained quite neutral in meaning, with no implication that such a ruler would necessarily exercise his power 'tyrannically') might appeal to the people when he challenged the constitutionally recognised authority of the oligarchs.

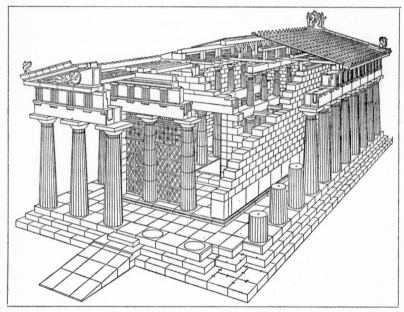

Constructional diagram of the Doric Temple of Aphaea in Aegina.

Tyrants appeared in many Greek cities, especially between about 650 and 550 B.C., and they often did much good. By breaking the entrenched privileges of the aristocracies they frequently paved the way for democracies. They helped the impoverished farmers, many of whom were drifting towards serfdom or even slavery, and they encouraged industry and trade. They aimed at peace and prosperity, and enriched their cities, providing them with temples and public buildings, and encouraging art and culture. Gradually, however, they became unpopular, and sometimes the tyrant himself or his sons became oppressive, so that no tyranny lasted longer than three generations or a century, and most were much briefer.

The word 'tyrant' was probably Lydian, and was first used in the Greek world by the Asiatic Greeks, some of whom entrusted their affairs to a tyrant, such as Thrasybulus of Miletus (ca. 610 B.C.), in order to organise their resistance to attack from the East by Lydia and then by Persia. Three cities in Greece which came under the rule of tyrants were those near the isthmus of Corinth, namely Corinth, Sicyon, and Megara. As we have seen, Corinth had already become prosperous and powerful under an oligarchical government, but this gave way about 650 B.C. to the rule of a tyrant, Cypselus; he and his son Periander (625–585) raised Corinth to new heights of prosperity. Fresh colonies were founded at Apollonia and Potidaea to give Corinth control of the main route across the Balkans, while at home Periander encouraged cultural as well as economic life, not least by developing the Isthmian Games. Tyrants had common interests which often led to friendship; thus Cypselus was friendly with Theagenes, the tyrant of Megara, and he in turn helped his son-in-law Cylon in an unsuccessful attempt to seize the tyranny atAthens.

So far nothing has been said about Athens, where there had been a My-cenaean settlement with a royal palace on the Acropolis. This older order was swept away during the Dorian invasion of Greece when Athens and Attica formed a place of refuge for the uprooted peoples, into which the Dorians did not penetrate. In Attica the pre-conquest Ionic dialect survived, and it was from here, too, that many of the Greeks crossed the seas to settle in Ionia. After these disturbed times, Athens very gradually absorbed the various independent settlements in Attica and unified the whole area in a single Athenian state. Tradition ascribed this slow process, which was completed about 700 B.C., to the hero Theseus. The people were divided into Brotherhoods (*phratriae*) and four Tribes (*phylae*), probably at first for purposes of war, while the aristocratic large land-owners were also grouped into exclusive Clans (*genē*). In early days the state was ruled by a king, who was advised by a council of nobles, the Areopagus; but gradually the king's power declined, and he was compelled to make way for an aristocracy, perhaps in the late eighth century. His former powers devolved upon three executive magistrates, the Archons, who later were assisted by six lesser officials (*Thesmothetae*). Military needs led to the division of the people into property classes according to their wealth: the *Hippeis* (Knights) who could serve as cavalry, the *Zeugitae* who could provide body-armour and serve as heavy-armed infantry (hoplites), and the *Thetes* (labourers). This last class was excluded from the meetings of a Popular Assembly (*Ecclesia*) which was allowed to meet but had very little political influence at this time; the nobles in the Areopagus controlled the state.

It was not very long before one of the nobles tried to seize power as tyrant; but this attempt by Cylon, who had won the foot-race at Olympia, was thwarted (ca. 636); neither the other nobles nor the peasants supported this revolutionary move. The people, however, gradually became more restless, demanding in particular to know the law, which the nobles alone administered. This demand for a law-giver resulted in entrusting the task to Draco (ca. 621), who drew up a code of laws which in themselves were not illiberal for these early days but which carried severe penalties for their infringement; hence they were said to have been written in blood. But soon the peasants of Attica found their economic and social difficulties increasingly burdensome. As the population grew, food became short, since apart from a few pockets of fertile land much of Attica was mountainous. Further, the introduction of coinage helped the rich, the merchant and industrial classes, but confused the poor, and many of the nobles began to exploit the ruined peasantry, so gaining control of an increasing share of the land. Thus many small farmers were forced into debt, serfdom, or even slavery. Before, however, this social discontent exploded into open revolution, the Athenians had the good sense to appoint a man to cope with the situation.

In 594 Solon received authority and declared a 'Shaking-off of Burdens'. The oppressed peasants were restored, and in the future no one was to raise a loan by offering his person as security. Beside encouraging agriculture, Solon promoted overseas trade, and to this end he reformed the standard of Athenian coinage. He also helped industry by granting citizenship to foreigners who settled in Attica and practised a trade. Further,

Minoan and Mycenaean civilisation. Extensive remains of Minoan culture—the earliest civilisation of Europe—can be found on the hill slopes of Crete. 13. View of the palace at Cnossus, residence of the legendary King Minos. 14. This aerial photograph shows the maze-like ground-plan of the palace, built round a central courtyard. Wall-paintings, pottery, seal-stones, etc. give an idea of the luxurious, civilised life led at court. 15. Representation of a bull attacked by a lion. 16. Vase with a motif of dolphins. 17. A tablet depicting a Minoan house. 18. Clay statuette of a bull. 19. The legend of the Minotaur slain by Theseus survived until classical Greek times, as is shown, for example, by this vase-painting of the 5th century B.C. 20. South wing of the palace of Cnossus with reconstructed portico. 21. North wing and (22) reconstructed colonnade of the palace.

13

14

15

16

17

18

19

20

21

22

23

24

25

26

27

28

29

30

31

he not only drew up a code of laws, but he published it where all could see it. He also realised the need for constitutional adjustment and reform, seeking for a fairer distribution of political powers between the nobles and people. He gave the lowest class, the Thetes, political rights: they became members of the Assembly and also of the new Popular Lawcourt (*Heliaea*) that Solon created. This new court could judge magistrates after their year of office, could prosecute for public offences, and formed a court of appeal for the people. The Areopagus lost some of its powers and became the guardian of the laws, while a new Council of 400 (*Boulē*) was created to discuss matters before they were presented to the Assembly. Since the Council was not open to the Thetes, it was a conservative body. What Solon sought was a balanced or moderate oligarchy in which the rights of the people would be protected; but his reforms paved the way for full democracy.

But the unity which Solon seemed to have established soon broke down, and to the rival interests of the nobles of the Plain and the traders of the Coast there were added the claims of the peasants of the Hill country. These last were led by a noble named Peisistratus, who managed to seize power as a tyrant and, after some vicissitudes, to hold it for some twenty years (546–527 B.C.). Like tyrants elsewhere, he improved the city and encouraged artistic and cultural development. Thus he founded the Dionysian Festival from which Athenian tragedy developed, and he improved the great Panathenaic state festival in honour of Athene, the patron goddess of the state; recitation of the Homeric poems became a regular feature of the festival. Further, he promoted agriculture (especially olive growing), helped the small farmer, and encouraged overseas trade. Thus Athens enjoyed a period of increasing prosperity, safeguarded by the skill with which Peisistratus protected its interests abroad through

Many other Minoan palaces have been found on Cretan sites, e.g. Phaestus (**23–24**), a city near the south coast, sheltered by a mountain ridge. A monumental staircase and walls still survive. **25.** Numerous remains of Mycenaean civilisation are still to be seen in the Peloponnese; palaces here were also fortresses, like the strategically situated Mycenae. **26.** Tiryns, a citadel-palace on an isolated hill; parts of its mighty walls (over 33 ft. high) and entrance gate are still preserved. **27.** Access to the citadel of Mycenae was through the Lion Gate, which has survived more than three millennia. **28.** The golden masks and other objects found by the German archaeologist Schliemann inside a grave circle (pl. 30) have yielded striking proof of the power of Mycenaean kings. **29.** Mycenaean soldiers. **30.** The grave circle behind the Lion Gate. **31.** The megaron of the palace.

alliances with other cities. After this enlightened despot died, power passed to his son Hippias, who after the murder of his brother feared for his own safety and ruled oppressively until he was overthrown by the rival family of the Alcmaeonidae, who persuaded Sparta to send a force to help them. But although the tyranny came to an end in 510, political control did not remain in the hands of the nobles. Despite further Spartan intervention, a democratic leader, Cleisthenes, won power and reformed the constitution in 508.

Cleisthenes smashed the power of the nobles, which was exercised through the Clan system, by abolishing the old Tribes and creating ten new ones, but in so artificial a manner that no single noble could dominate a whole tribe; rather, each tribe now represented the mixed interests of nobles, traders, and farmers. Also all the resident aliens (*Metoikoi* or metics) who had settled in Athens since Solon's day were now incorporated in the parishes ('demes') which Cleisthenes re-organised. Henceforth every Athenian citizen was a member of a deme; such membership passed from father to son; and a man became known as A, the son of B, of X deme. Cleisthenes also re-organised the Council (*Boulē*) on the basis of the new tribes. It comprised 500 members, chosen by lot from selected demesmen, and in order to make it efficient it was divided into ten Committees of fifty members (*Prytanies*), one of which was always in session throughout the year. The main task of the Council was to prepare business for the Assembly of all the citizens, the Ecclesia, which was obviously too large to manage without a smaller body to help it. The importance of the Council, in which all citizens over thirty years old might serve, can scarcely be exaggerated: it alone made possible the functioning of a democratic system. Thus Cleisthenes' reforms made Athens a democracy. After a half-hearted attempt by Sparta to interfere in its internal affairs, Athens was allowed to develop on its own lines. The next challenge came not from another Greek city, but from the great Persian Empire.

EARLY GREEK CIVILISATION

The traditional lays, which were ultimately fused into the *Iliad* and *Odyssey* (p. 26), had been sung by minstrels in the courts of kings and nobles in Ionia, and it was among the Asiatic Greeks that a fine flowering of lyric poetry and philosophical inquiry developed. Poets abandoned the epic and the hexameter and began to write personal poetry, describing their own feelings and lives, in elegiac and iambic metres. Archilochus of Paros was noted for his bitterness, and Alcaeus of Lesbos (ca. 600 B.C.) wrote lyric poems on love, wine, and politics, while his younger contemporary Sappho found inspiration in the worship of Aphrodite and the Muses for poems of deep personal feeling and beauty. Meantime on the Greek mainland the Homeric tradition had been continued, though in very different vein, by Hesiod, whose father had migrated from Aeolis to Boeotia (perhaps ca. 800 B.C.). Here in a poor village Hesiod struggled with the difficulties of a farmer's life, which he described in his poem, *Works and Days;* he preached a gospel of hard and honest work. In his *Theogony* he described the generations of the gods and tried to bring them into line with his ideas of the universe as a whole; he believed in the ultimate triumph of justice and that the universe was based on order. The growth of the various national festivals in Greece (e.g. at Olympia and Delphi) promoted another form of poetry, hymns in hexameter verse to individual deities, which were sung in competitions; several of these survive in a collection known as the *Homeric Hymns.* In the worship of the gods, music and dance were linked with song, and choral and processional songs were composed for the festivals. Thus Alcman wrote lyrical poems for choirs of maidens in early Sparta, where Tyrtaeus composed war-songs and elegies. The poems of Theognis of Megara reflect the distaste of an aristocratic society at the rise of a commercial class, while at Athens in elegiac verse Solon described and justified his reforms and stressed man's individual and social responsibilities: honour, not wealth, is the goal of life. Thus the early Greek world saw the growth of a wealth of poetry, of which only a fraction has survived. The *Iliad* and *Odyssey* have ever since held a unique place in the poetry of the world; and while some of the mainland poets reflect the religious ideas and the corporate spirit of their cities, the work of the eastern Greeks was marked by a strong individualism.

The artistic achievements of the early Greeks were scarcely less brilliant and diversified. In the seventh century a great advance was made beyond the formal and somewhat mechanical work of the 'geometric period'. This was due largely to the stimulus from contacts with the East. In pottery increasing skill was shown in drawing and decoration, and many local styles of great excellence developed, at Corinth, Sparta, Rhodes, and Chios. By 600 B.C. the black-figure style had been evolved at Athens, and during the century Athenian wares began to oust their rivals in the markets of the Mediterranean. About 525 a new technique, the red-figure, was introduced at Athens, which allowed artists to cast off all early archaic stiffness and to pass to the classical style of the fifth century. No less skilful were the engravers of the dies for the multiplicity of coin types which the various cities demanded. The seventh century also saw the development of both architecture and sculpture. In architecture the chief forms or 'orders' were the Doric in Greece, Magna Graecia, and Sicily, and the Ionic which spread from Asia Minor to some mainland centres such as Athens and Delphi; thus most Greek cities were now adorned with temples and other buildings. In sculpture many styles developed, e.g. a Doric in the Peloponnese and Crete, a softer style in the eastern islands and Ionia, and in the sixth century Athens had its own school of sculpture, noted for its *kouroi* (young male figures) and *kourai* (maidens). The stiffness of these archaic styles often developed into a brilliant gaiety. Much of this early art was inspired by religious conceptions, and figures of the gods were among the chief works of sculpture.

Greek religion was the concern of both the family and the state: family worship of Hestia, the goddess of the hearth, was paralleled in the state worship of Hestia and the city's patron deity, while family ritual connected with birth, marriage, and death had its counterpart in the ritual acts of worship before public ceremonies. It is noteworthy, however, that Greek religion differs in some basic ways from what is generally regarded as constituting religion in the modern world. Thus in general Greek religion imposed no creed and no system of morality: although certain actions might be considered to be displeasing to the gods, a man's private morals and beliefs were not the concern of the state or of a priesthood, provided that he did not try to subvert the established forms of worship. While each city had its own cults, the common possession of the Homeric

32. In the period of early Greek culture in which the Homeric epic was created, bards and minstrels went from court to court reciting heroic poetry. 33–4. Terracottas from Boeotia bear witness to life about 600 B.C.: Women preparing dough (33); a horse (34). Early bronzes from the Peloponnese and S. Italy excel in design and execution: horseman (35) and girl running (36). Early pottery was decorated with 'geometric' patterns: part of a vase showing a scene set between a pattern of lines (37). 38–9. Early black-figure pottery: the design is in black on a lighter background. 40–1. Characteristic of early sculpture is the frontal style, employed particularly for *kouroi* and *kourai* figures, of which the 'archaic smile' (42–3) is also typical. 44. Early bronze head of Zeus, from Olympia.

KA⅃ONE

32

33

34

35

36

37

38

39

40

41

42

43

44

45

46

47

48

50

51

53

54

55

poems tended to create a general devotion to the Olympian gods. Interest in the gods was furthered by the extraordinary richness of Greek mythology: their mytho-poetic facility, which came into play in order to explain some real or imaginary phenomena, created one of the most complex sets of images and symbols for many aspects of experience that the imagination of man has devised. But men soon began to desire more personal forms of worship, which found expression in the cults of Demeter and Dionysus. The former was worshipped at Eleusis, where those initiated into the Mysteries could watch rites which re-enacted the story of Demeter and her daughter Persephone, who had to spend part of each year in the Underworld, thus symbolising the annual death and resurrection of the seasons. By ritual purification the initiates could hope for personal survival after death, and the cult was available not only for Athenians but for all Greeks, including women and even slaves. The worship of Dionysus, which came to Greece from Thrace, was much wilder: during midnight orgies its followers in ecstatic frenzies devoured raw flesh. When introduced into Greece, some of the wilder features were modified. It was also linked with the cult of Orpheus, whose followers developed a religion and theology that was widely propagated, not least by Pythagoras of Samos who went to Italy and settled at Croton, where he founded an Orphic brotherhood (ca. 530 B.C.). The chief features of the sect were a belief in the transmigration of souls and an ascetic manner of life.

The mystery religions sought to find an answer to the problem of human existence. A totally different approach to this same basic question was that of philosophical inquiry, based on belief in the power of human reason. Greek thinkers in Asia Minor began boldly to inquire into the nature of the physical universe. The fact that they found differing answers is less important than that the inquirers asked the question and supposed

The Doric style of architecture, the first to attain full development, spread all over the Mediterranean. 46–7. Interior and exterior of Doric temples at (46) and Paestum (47). 48. The Doric temple of Aphaea in Aegina. 49. Tympana and friezes of temples gave sculptors opportunity to work out aesthetic problems. Dying warrior, corner figure on tympanum of the Temple of Aphaea. A climax in Greek history is the war with Persia. 50. The scene of the first great clash: the plain of Marathon. 51. A later momentous occasion was the battle of Thermopylae. 52. Success in the battle in the narrows round Salamis brought Greece final victory at sea. 53. Helmeted hoplite. Two aspects of Greece: races during funeral games (54) and widely extended trade, as shown by a large 6th cent B.C. krater found in central France (55).

that some unifying principle could be discovered. Thales of Miletus early in the sixth century found this principle in water, Anaximenes in air; Pythagoras made important discoveries in mathematics and astronomy, believing number to be the basis of the world; Xenophanes of Colophon rejected traditional religious beliefs and found the first principle in a god who was identified with the whole cosmos and who moved all things by his mind. Heracleitus of Ephesus (ca. 500) believed in perpetual change, with all things becoming and passing away. Parmenides of Elea in Italy, however, argued that only an unchangeable One existed and that the world of sense was only appearance. All these early probings into the meaning of life and the universe were among the greatest achievements of the Greek spirit and prevented the Greek world from falling under the deadening influence of a formal state religion. They demonstrated that the true basis of scientific inquiry must be rational thought.

GREECE AND PERSIA

A great change was taking place in the East during the seventh and sixth centuries: political control was passing from the Semitic peoples to those of Indo-European origin. About 700 B.C. the Medes managed to throw off the yoke of Assyria and assert their independence. After a period of consolidation they moved to the attack, and with the help of Babylonia they captured Nineveh in 612 and brought the Assyrian Empire to an end. Next they advanced into the eastern part of Asia Minor and clashed with the kingdom of Lydia, which had been built up by Gyges (ca. 685–652). After a battle, which was broken off because of an eclipse of the sun, a frontier was established between the two kingdoms at the river Halys (585 B.C.); it is noteworthy that Thales of Miletus (see above) had predicted this eclipse.

The future, however, lay not with the conquering Medes, but with another Indo-European people, the kindred Persians who lived in the hilly district northeastward of the Persian Gulf. Under the leadership of their king Cyrus they expanded with astounding rapidity, and the other great kingdoms went down like nine-pins before them. They conquered Media in 549, Croesus the king of Lydia in 546, and Babylon in 538; in 525 Cyrus' successor, Cambyses, overcame Egypt. This vast new power was organised by Darius, who came to the throne in 521. His

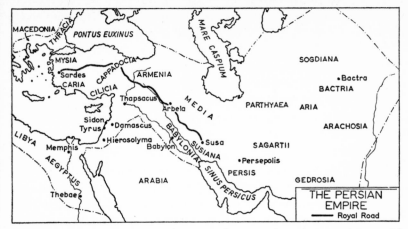

kingdom stretched from northwest India to Asia Minor, and it could
be held together only by a carefully devised provincial system and constant vigilance. The Empire was divided into some twenty or more
satrapies, in each of which the satrap (governor) was checked by an independent general appointed by the king. Further, in order to facilitate the
speedy movement of information and troops, the road system was developed in a way that astonished the Greeks: Herodotus was greatly im-
pressed with the great Royal Road that ran for 1,500 miles from the
capital Susa to Sardes. All authority was vested in the king, whom the
Greeks regarded as The King, the type and symbol of an absolute monarch
whose power was alien to their ideas of freedom. Despite this, however,
in many respects the Persians were enlightened and advanced in civilisation, and in return for obligations that were not unduly oppressive they
gave their subjects peace and security.

These great changes in the East naturally soon began to affect the Greeks
of Asia Minor, whose early achievements have already been noted. In
the seventh century they had been attacked by the Lydians, and later
most of them had been reduced by Croesus (ca. 560–546), to whom they
had to pay tribute; but they retained considerable freedom and their
trade increased, helped by the use of coinage, a device that they like
the other Greeks borrowed from Lydia. After Lydia had succumbed to
Persia, the Greek cities were before long reduced by Cyrus; they were
not enslaved, but they had to pay tribute, supply troops, and appoint
tyrants who were acceptable to Persia. Thus Asia Minor was absorbed
into the Persian Empire. Samos under Polycrates held out until ca. 524,

while some of the Phocaeans fled to Corsica to seek a new home in the West.

Would Darius be satisfied to remain in Asia or would he turn to Europe and the kinsmen of his Greek subjects? The Greeks do not appear to have been unduly worried, although his next act was certainly not very reassuring: he crossed the Bosporus into Europe, advanced to the Ister (Danube) and made a demonstration against the Scythians in southern Russia (ca. 512 B.C.). This expedition was a failure; but Darius left behind him an army to reduce at least the coastal area of Thrace. The next move came from the Ionian Greeks. Increasingly discontented for political and economic reasons, they decided to revolt from Persia, despite the fact that all the support that they could extract from Greece was twenty ships from Athens and five from Eretria; Sparta refused them any help (499). At first they were not unsuccessful, and the revolt spread; but they failed to unite adequately or to make full use of their sea power. Finally, in 494, the Persians moved to the offensive; they destroyed the Greek fleet off Lade and carried Miletus by storm. Thus the revolt was crushed, but on the whole the Ionians were let off lightly: as the pro-Persian tyrants had proved unsuccessful the Persians now set up democracies in the Greek cities. However, the trade and culture of the Asiatic Greeks began to decline.

Darius then sent an expedition in 492 to occupy Thrace and Macedon, but it met with disaster: the fleet was wrecked at Mount Athos and the land army was assailed by a Thracian tribe. Whether, if successful in its first objective, the expedition would have moved on against Greece proper can hardly be established, but Darius certainly decided to take further action. As the co-operation of his army and navy had failed, he decided on a smaller expedition by sea, which was aimed in the first

The Age of Pericles. Athens, the most important city in the history of Greece, grew up around a 515 ft. hill in Attica. This hill, the Acropolis, 920 ft. long, still dominates the city. 56 and 57 show a reconstruction and the present ruins 56 shows the Acropolis as it appeared in classical times, with its surroundings as they were in Roman times. The Parthenon (58) dominated the Acropolis. 59. Coin of Athens with the owl sacred to Athena. Sculpture attained its zenith at this period. 60. Horse's head from the eastern pediment of the Parthenon. 61. Equestrian group from the N. frieze. 62. Plaque from Melos, probably showing Aphrodite. 63. The 'Fair-haired Ephebe', ca. 480 B.C., is typical of the transition from the earlier style to classical refinement.

56

57

58

59

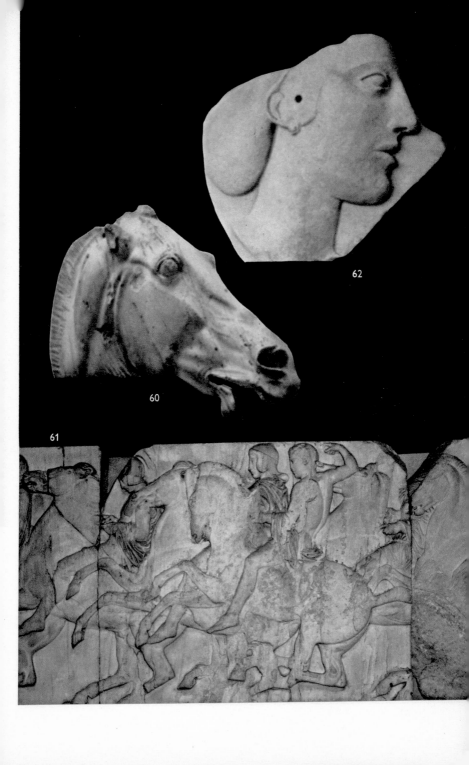

62

60

61

64

65

67

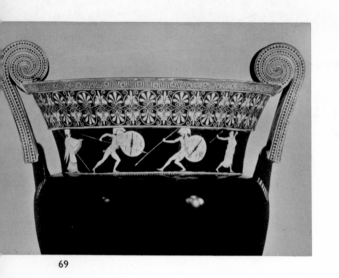

69

70

71

instance only at Athens and Eretria in order to punish them for the very limited support that they had given to the Ionian Greeks in their revolt. In 490 the expedition crossed the Aegean, captured Eretria, and landed at Marathon on the coast of Attica. The Athenian army marched out to meet the enemy. Both sides waited a few days, the Athenians because they hoped for help from Sparta (it did not come in time, and Athens had to fight unaided except by the little town of Plataea), the Persians because they hoped that traitors in Athens might hand over the city to them and that then they could reinstate Hippias as tyrant and as their agent. The Athenian army, finding that the Persians were sending part of their force round by sea against Athens itself, launched their attack on the superior numbers of the enemy. When the battle was over, 6,400 Persians lay on the field, and only 192 Athenians. It was an incredible victory; the Persians accepted the verdict and the survivors sailed for home.

Darius, however, could hardly allow the Persian Empire to be defeated by the men of a single city-state without seeking revenge. This he planned; but it was left to Xerxes, who succeeded him in 484, to implement his plans. This time there must be no failure. Great forces must be sent by land and sea. While the army marched along the coast, it would be covered and supplied by the fleet which sailed alongside. The Hellespont was bridged, a canal was cut though the neck of Athos, and depots of food were laid up on the route. At length in the spring of 480 Xerxes was ready, and the expedition crossed the Hellespont into Europe.

Most of the Greeks were slow to face the reality of their mortal danger. But one man at least had the foresight to anticipate and prepare, the Athenian Themistocles. He had gradually gained political control in the 480s, and in particular he had persuaded the Athenians to build a great

The Erechtheum (64) and the temple of Nike (65), both built on the Acropolis and in the Doric style, are important architectural achievements. 66. Later copy of Athena, by Myron, one of the great sculptors of the age of Pericles. The city of Athens was embellished with numerous buildings on and around the Acropolis, including many in the Agora. None of the latter survives nearly intact except the temple of Hephaestus (67). The Agora boasted several stoas where much public business was conducted. The recently rebuilt Stoa of Attalus, originally erected in the middle of the 3rd cent. B.C., gives some idea of these porticos. 68. Interior of this stoa. 69. In vase-painting the black-figure style was succeeded by the red-figure: rim of a krater, ca. 490 B.C. 70. White funerary lekythos of the same period. 71. Bowl decorated with female dancers and musicians in rich flowing robes.

fleet for use in a war against Aegina in which they were engaged, but Themistocles in fact had the Persian menace in mind. But how were the Greeks, with their inferior numbers, to resist? First, they must unite, always a difficult decision for Greeks. Those who were willing to fight sent envoys to a meeting where a League was formed under the leadership of Sparta, to whom the Athenians nobly surrendered the supreme command by land and sea. But the Confederacy had many gaps: Argos would not join, and Boeotia and Thessaly could not be trusted very far. As to strategy, clearly the geography of Greece must be turned to the best advantage. If the Persian army could be held up in a narrow pass, where its vast numbers would be unavailing, perhaps the fleet might be tempted into narrow waters and there be challenged. If only it could be defeated, then the army would be unlikely to stay in Greece in overwhelming force. So it was decided to try to hold the Vale of Tempe, or failing that, the pass of Thermopylae; meanwhile the Persian fleet might venture in the narrow waters between Euboea and the mainland. But Spartan hopes were not high, and they probably wanted to make the main defence line at the isthmus of Corinth; even Athens prepared for the worst, if in fact (as a recently discovered inscription suggests) Themistocles at this point carried a decree providing for an orderly evacuation of the city if it became necessary. The plans were, however, adopted; but the attempt to hold Tempe was soon abandoned, and Thessaly went over to Persia. The Greeks then occupied Thermopylae, but the Spartans did not commit their full forces. When the Persians attacked, the Greeks hurled back all their attempts until a traitor showed the Persians a mountain track that would lead them round to the rear of the Greeks. Even so, the Spartan commander Leonidas tried to hold out a day longer, hoping to give the Greek fleet a further chance to win a victory. The fleet, which was stationed at Artemisium in the north of Euboea, had been lucky in that a storm had wrecked a portion of the Persian navy, but the surviving squadrons were still strong enough to fight the Greek ships to a stand-still. So in fact Leonidas' last stand, in which he and his 300 Spartans fought until all perished, proved of no decisive military value. When the Greek fleet learned that Thermopylae had fallen, it retired southwards to Salamis.

The Persian army quickly overran central Greece, and then occupied Athens, including the Acropolis, from which the women, children, and the old had already been evacuated to Salamis and other centres. All Athenian hopes now rested on the fleet, to which they contributed 180 ships out of a total of 366. In fear that the Spartans would not fight at Salamis but retire within the Peloponnese, Themistocles even risked sending an apparently treacherous message to Xerxes, which induced him to attack the Greek fleet immediately in the narrow straits between the island of Salamis and the mainland of Attica. Here the relatively small Greek fleet won its decisive victory. Not only was southern Greece now saved, but the whole Persian strategy, which was based on co-operation of army and navy, was smashed. Xerxes went back to Asia, leaving behind an effective land army, which the Greeks brought to battle and defeat at Plataea in the summer of 479. The Persian forces fled from Greece, and the victorious Greeks lost no time in punishing Thebes which had 'Medised'. Meantime the Greek fleet had ventured across the Aegean and defeated the Persian fleet and a land army at Mycale on the coast of Asia Minor. The Ionian Greeks, serving in the Persian force, went over to their fellow Greeks: 'thus Ionia revolted from the Persians a second time'.

The national victory must have seemed almost miraculous: a few independent city-states, who even in the hour of extreme danger co-operated with great reluctance, had humbled the might of the great Persian Empire. An upsurge of confidence inspired many; but grave tasks remained. Athens was a pile of ruins, the Asiatic Greeks must be saved from Persian revenge, and there was the risk that Persia might one day return to the attack even against Greece itself. The Greeks would naturally look to Sparta to continue that leadership which it had exercised during the war, but Sparta was not eager or suited. It had few interests outside the Peloponnese, and was not a naval power. After a halfhearted attempt to stop Athens from rebuilding its walls and another halfhearted effort to keep the lead at sea, the Spartans resigned the latter to the Athenians, who undertook to organise a means to protect the outlying Greeks. This was done through the formation of the Confederacy of Delos, an entirely voluntary league of allies, whose object was mutual protection and the ravaging of Persian territory, and whose headquarters were in the island of Delos. The allies provided either ships to the common fleet or else an equivalent money payment which was arranged equitably by an Athenian, Aristeides the Just. Under the energetic leadership of the Athenian Cimon the forces of the Confederacy won several successes, culminating in a great land and sea victory near the river Eurymedon in southwestern Asia Minor (ca. 467 B.C.). For some years thereafter Athens and Persia did not clash; but when Egypt revolted from Persia the Athenians decided to send 200 ships to help the rebels. After some initial success the rebellion was crushed, and a high proportion of the Athenian forces perished (454 B.C.). This great disaster was a blow which has a most serious effect on Athenian manpower and resources. But a few years later Cimon persuaded the Athenians to resume hostilities with Persia, and their forces won a notable victory in Cyprus. This resulted in a settlement, which was probably embodied in a formal peace (negotiated on the Athenian side by Callias) under which Persia promised not to sail into the Aegean or attack the Greek cities in Asia Minor, while

the Athenians were to respect the King's territory, in which Cyprus was now included. The object for which the Delian Confederacy had been formed was now achieved.

It is possible only to make brief reference to the fortunes of the Greeks in the West. Those in Sicily were exposed to constant pressure from the Carthaginians who were settled in the western end of the island, while many Greeks in southern Italy faced attack from the natives of the interior. Tyranny had emerged in many cities. In particular Gelon had built up the power of Syracuse, and was friendly with Theron of Acragas (Agrigentum).

Against this expanding coalition Anaxilas of Rhegium, who had occupied Messene, called in the help of the Carthaginians, who sent a large expedition from Africa. Thus while the eastern Greeks were fighting for their lives against Persia, their western kinsmen faced a Punic menace. This, however, was smashed at the battle of Himera (480 B.C.), while in 474 Gelon's successor, Hieron, defeated the Etruscans by sea off Cumae and thus saved the Greeks of Italy from this threat from the north. The economic and cultural achievements of these Western Greeks were of the highest order. Their cities were adorned with fine temples and other public buildings, and the courts of the tyrants were princely. Their culture is best reflected in the hymns of Pindar of Thebes, who, like many other famous poets, visited Sicily and received the patronage of the tyrants whose victories in the Pan-Hellenic Games of Greece the poet celebrated in his odes. In this highly-wrought verse we find great sympathy for the aristocratic ideals of men who sought excellence (*aretē*) in war or sport for the honour of their family or state. But notwithstanding the magnificence of Pindar's verse, he was depicting a society whose day was drawing to a close. The future lay with the democracy that he despised.

THE AGE OF PERICLES

The relations of Athens and the allies gradually changed, and ultimately what had been a voluntary alliance developed into an Athenian empire which many of its members resented. The first sign of change was in 472 when Carystus in Euboea was compelled to join the Confederacy. Then in 469 Naxos tried to secede, to be followed in 465 by Thasos. Athens regarded these movements as revolt, and both islands were reduced to subjection. The majority of the allies were of course still free, but the balance was gradually tilting in favour of the leader of the Confederacy.

Before long Athens' relations with Sparta also deteriorated. A devastating earthquake at Sparta in 464 gave the Messenian helots a chance to revolt. When the Spartans unexpectedly rejected some military help from Athens, which they themselves had first asked for, Athens broke off relations, and soon made alliances with Sparta's old enemy Argos and with Megara and Thessaly. This new balance of power before long led to war. At first this was between Athens and Corinth (459–8), but soon Sparta was involved. To counter Spartan intervention in Boeotia the Athenians sent an army there in 457 and after being checked by the Spartans at the battle of Tanagra defeated the Boeotians, with the result that Boeotia and Phocis became their allies. Thus besides a naval hegemony Athens now also controlled what was in effect a land empire, but only for ten years. In 447 Boeotia broke away, and this was followed by the revolt of Euboea and Megara. This was soon crushed; but the strain of fighting Sparta and Persia and trying to control central Greece had proved too taxing for Athens. In 445 it concluded a Thirty Years' Peace with Sparta. Each recognised the authority of the other, that of Athens at sea and of Sparta by land.

Athens' control of the allies was now tightened up, and when one of the strongest, the island of Samos, tried to revolt in 440, it was crushed; how much less chance, then, had the smaller states. One method by which Athens controlled its empire was through the establishment of colonies (*cleruchies*) of its own citizens at strategic points. Thus about 447 B.C. cleruchies were sent out to Euboea, the Thracian Chersonese, Naxos, and Andros, while ten years later Pericles led an Athenian fleet into the Propontis (Sea of Marmora) and the Euxine (Black Sea), where some more settlements were made and good relations established with the Cimmerian Bosporus (the Crimea), on which area Athens increasingly depended for corn supply. In 443 a pan-Hellenic colony was established under Athenian leadership at Thurii in south Italy, while in 437 Athens sent a colony to Amphipolis. Other grievances of the allies, in addition to the cleruchies, were that they were compelled to use Athenian coinage (the treasury had already been transferred from Delos to Athens in 454), to submit certain legal cases for trial to Athens, to endure some interference in their internal affairs (e.g. the establishment of democracies, especially in cases of revolt), and to continue to pay their annual contribution to the Confederacy, which they now regarded as tribute exacted by an imperial mistress. On the other hand, many of them were doubtless reasonably satisfied, and all got a real return for their money in peace and protection from Persia.

The policy of Athens at this time was directed by Pericles. He had come to political power in the wake of some democratic constitutional reforms which had been introduced at various dates around the middle of the century. The political power of the Areopagus was still further limited, the archonship had been opened to the third Solonian class (the Zeugitae), and the principle of pay for public office had been introduced. This was given at first to the jurymen (dicasts), but was gradually extended to other services (such as magistracies and members of the Council); it was envisaged

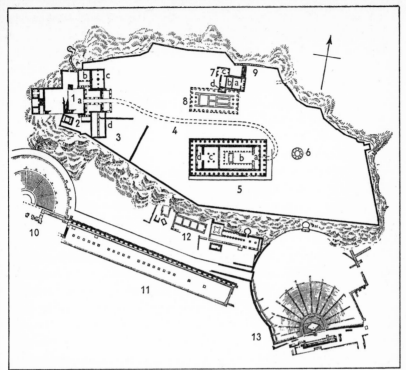

Plan of the Acropolis. 1. Propylaea: A, entrance gate; B, gallery; C,D, uncompleted portions. 2. Temple of Nike. 3. Demesne of Artemis. 4. Sacred way. 5. Partenon: A, outer hall; B, cella, with representations of the gods; C, treasure chamber; D, inner hall. 6. Roman temple. 7. Erechtheum: A, cella of Athena; B, cella of Erechtheus; C, north hall; D, porch of the caryatids. 8. Site of the Hekatompedon. 9. Part of the ancient walls, with remains of columns. 10. Odeion of Atticus. 11. Stoa of Eumenes II. 12. Sanctuary of Asclepius. 13. Theatre of Dionysus.

not as a payment for the performance of civic duty, but rather as an allowance, so that no citizen should be prevented from doing his duty through poverty. Later moralists, such as Plato, regarded it as a retrograde step.

Pericles further wished to make Athens a worthy capital of the empire, and he promoted a building programme which resulted in the creation of many great temples and works of art that have ever since made Athens famous, such as the new Parthenon, with its cult statue of Athene made by Pheidias, the statue of Athene Promachos on the Acropolis, the Propylaea, and many others. Much of the money to finance this came from the tribute of the allies. Pericles could argue that not only had the Persians destroyed the temples at Athens and that therefore to rebuild them was a legitimate use of funds devoted to an anti-Persian cause, but also that Athens was in fact providing protection from the Persians. The allies' complaints were voiced by Pericles' opponent Thucydides (son of Melesias, not the historian), but when the latter was ostracised in 443 Pericles was left supreme in Athens, without a serious political rival. He was repeatedly re-elected to the office of *strategos*. 'In name Athens was a democracy, in fact it was governed by its foremost citizen.' So Thucydides the historian might write. But it is well to recall that Pericles' power rested only on his ability to hold the confidence of the people; as soon as they began to distrust him, they could at once stop re-electing him to an annual office. It was his own natural abilities, his incorruptibility, and his wise guidance that kept him in power.

The material prosperity of Athens increased. As the centre of an Aegean empire in which free trade flourished, it drew to itself the commerce of a wide area, especially in the years of peace after 446. All classes benefited. The landed aristocracy had capital to invest; many new families gained wealth through trade and contracting; the middle class (the Zeugitae) in particular increased and prospered, farmers, craftsmen, and traders alike; while the lowest class (the Thetes) had many means of increasing their resources (such as state pay and casual labour at harvest time). Further, there was a large class of prosperous resident aliens (the metics) who brought wealth to the state; although they lacked political rights, they enjoyed great economic and social freedom. The population of slaves also increased. They provided both skilled and unskilled labour, and their conditions varied enormously: those who worked in the state mines suffered greatly, but the lot of many in the city was not unbearable, since they had certain legal rights and they were not differentiated by any special dress from the free men alongside whom they might work. Thus Athens was a mixed community, in which there was a privileged citizen body (probably

Sanctuaries were numerous and cults spread far and wide from them. From very early times Olympia was especially important as a sanctuary of Zeus and scene of the Olympic games, where Greeks competed with each other in many forms of sport. 72. Javelin-thrower preparing for the throw. 73. Four runners. 74. The sanctuary at Olympia, with the great temple of Zeus and other sacred buildings. 75. Delphi, centre of the worship of Apollo. In the middle is superimposed a reconstruction of the Temple of Apollo, with treasuries. 76. Stadium at Delphi with view of the countryside. 77. Delos, birthplace of Apollo and Artemis. 78. Relief, probably 5th cent. B.C., showing Apollo, Artemis, and Leto with Nike (right) before a temple in Delos. Epidaurus. Here the sick came to ask Asclepius for healing. 79. Votive relief, probably dedicated to Asclepius. 80. The theatre at Epidaurus.

72

73

74

75

76

79

80

81

82

83   84

85

86

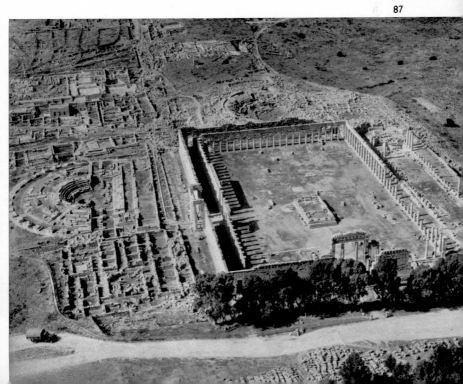

87

a little under half the population). Among the citizens, however, there was almost complete political equality, and freedom of speech and thought was untrammelled. The democratic constitution gave to such a large proportion of the citizens personal experience and responsibility in managing the affairs of the state that even an Assembly of all the citizens could, aided by the 'committee' of the Council, function with moderation and efficiency: the will of the people determined the action of the state. And Pericles could justly hold up this ideal to his fellow-citizens as a cause for love and admiration, and to the rest of the Greeks as a worthy example and pattern.

The achievements of the Periclean age in art showed all men that the Acropolis was not only the religious centre of the city but also the crowning glory of its power and artistic genius. Some of its temples and sculptures, the work of such men as Ictinus and Pheidias, have already been mentioned. The nobility and pre-eminent skill of the sculptured frieze of the Parthenon, which depicted the procession of the Athenian people at the Panathenaic Festival, and of the figures of gods from the pediments, are still reflected in the sadly mutilated pieces that survive. Nor was Athens the only city to benefit from this artistic output. Sculptors and architects moved freely in Greece, and the statue of Zeus that Pheidias made at Olympia was regarded as one of the greatest works of the ancient world. Similarly the bronze statues by Polycleitus, following in the traditions of the Peloponnesian school, were universally regarded. So too the works of the great painter Polygnotus were to be found in other cities besides Athens.

As art transcended city boundaries, so did the creative mind of Herodotus, who was born in Halicarnassus, lived in Samos, resided in Athens, and became a citizen of the colony founded at Thurii in 443. 'The father of history' wanted to preserve for future generations some knowledge of the great deeds 'accomplished by Greeks and non-Greeks, and especially why

81. The theatre of Dionysus at Athens, dating back to the 6th cent., where many first performances of works by Aeschylus, Sophocles, etc., took place. 82. Scene from a modern performance of *Oedipus Rex* at Delphi. Numerous scenes have been recorded on reliefs, vases, etc. 83. Actor dressed as a woman, with a mask in his hand. 84. Performance of *Iphigenia*. 85. Many vase-paintings indicate the important rôle of music: men playing lyres. 86. All round the Mediterranean Greek colonies promoted trade. 87. Cyrene, a trade centre in North Africa with numerous Greek and Roman remains. 88. The acropolis of Lindus in Rhodes is a striking example of this prominent and central feature of many Greek cities. 89. Syracuse, one of the greatest cities in the West, a centre of politics, learning, and commerce, was founded on an island and spread to the mainland.

they went to war with one another'. Thus his *History* is both an account of much of the known world, in which Herodotus himself had travelled widely with keen eyes and inquiring mind, and also of the Persian Wars and their cultural and political background. This was a tremendous achievement, the more so because it is set forth in a style of the utmost charm and direct appeal.

Many would claim that the greatest achievement of the fifth century was the flowering of Attic tragedy, which was rooted in religion. Plays were produced at a state festival in honour of Dionysus, and the great dramas show not only the genius of the poets but also the taste of the Athenian people who formed the audience. This new form of art first appeared about 534 B.C. and was developed into a blending of dialogue and choral lyrics by Aeschylus (ca. 525–456 B.C.). In his dramas, within the framework of contemporary religious beliefs, he wrestled with fundamental problems of man's suffering and the individual's relations to his family, his country, and the universe. While Aeschylus belongs rather to the period of the Persian Wars (he himself fought at Marathon and Salamis), his younger contemporary Sophocles (ca. 496–406) reflects the spirit of the age of Pericles, whose colleague he was as general in 440. Like his predecessor, Sophocles took his subject-matter from the heroic legends of the Greeks, whence he drew examples of the nobility of man faced by a fate which he could not avert but which he could meet with heroism. He shows the individual struggling between the claims of the man-made law of his city and the dictates of his conscience which derived from laws that are 'unchangeable, unwritten, and everlasting'. Such universal themes, which still harass the minds and souls of men, show that the poet, although in harmony with the ordinary religious ideas of his day, was at the same time alert to the problems that a more critical age was beginning to pose.

One of the more advanced thinkers was a friend and teacher of Pericles, Anaxagoras, who settled in Athens from Clazomenae and developed a materialistic theory of the universe. He explained all material objects as composed of 'seeds' or particles; these are controlled by Mind, but he regarded Mind itself as only a specialised form of matter. Such views led on to the creation of an atomic theory, that the universe consists of atoms and void. This was originated by Leucippus of Miletus (ca. 440 B.C.) and developed by Democritus of Abdera (ca. 460–370). The views of Anaxagoras differed greatly from those of Empedocles of Acragas (ca. 493–433), who postulated four basic elements which were activated by Love and Strife, and from those of Zeno of Elea, who was concerned with the problem of motion. All this scientific inquiry, which was based upon thought rather than experiment, created a desire for more knowledge, not least for 'higher education' for the young men of Athens. This need was met by travelling teachers, known as Sophists. One of the earliest to teach at Athens was Pericles' friend Protagoras from Abdera, who believed in the relativity and subjectivity of knowledge ('Man is the measure of all things'), and was agnostic in the matter of belief in the gods. The story that he was tried for impiety and that his works were burned is of doubtful historicity, but it reflects the changing climate of thought that was beginning to make itself felt during the Periclean age.

ATHENS AND SPARTA

These two cities provided an extraordinary contrast. While the Athenians developed their intellectual and artistic life and beautified their city, the Spartans remained shut off from the rest of the Greek world, with no art or literature, no fine buildings, no development in their social, political, or constitutional life. Sparta continued as a 'fossilised' military state, although its great military qualities and stable constitution provoked the admiration of some other Greeks, including certain aristocratic intellectual circles in Athens itself. The increasing power of Athens and the resentment that it caused finally led to a breakdown of the Thirty Years' Peace (see p. 70) and to the Peloponnesian War (431–404), which shook the whole Greek world to its foundations.

At first Corinth, a trade rival to Athens, was more alarmed at Athenian power than was Sparta, but Pericles believed that war would come and he prepared for it. It was precipitated by two episodes. First, Athens supported Corcyra in a quarrel against its own mother-city of Corinth (433), and secondly another colony of Corinth, Potidaea, which was a member of the Athenian empire, revolted from Athens and was put under siege. Corinth soon persuaded Sparta and its Peloponnesian allies that the time had come to challenge Athens, and in 431 they invaded Attica.

A struggle between a land power and a sea power must present particular difficulties. Pericles' strategy was to avoid pitched battles and withdraw the population of Attica into the city of Athens (linked, since 457, with the Piraeus by the Long Walls) while the enemy were devastating the countryside; when they withdrew, the Athenians must use their naval power to strike where it would hurt most. The vicissitudes of the war cannot be traced here. It is enough to say that Pericles' plan was thwarted by a plague which struck down Athens in 430 and lasted three years, destroying perhaps a third of the population. Despite this, Athens showed great activity in various fields, at Potidaea, in northwest Greece, in Lesbos, in Corcyra, and in checking the annual invasion of Attica by the Peloponnesians. In 425 the Athenians occupied a strong point on the Peloponnesian coast at Pylos, where they inflicted a severe setback on the Spartans, thanks partly to the lead of Cleon, a demagogue who advocated greater daring. This departure from the policy of Pericles, who had died in 429, was not happy. Athens was defeated in Boeotia and lost Amphipolis, where Cleon was killed in an attempt to regain it. By 421 both sides were ready to negotiate a peace, which was arranged on the Athenian side by Nicias. When some of Sparta's allies refused to join in, Athens and Sparta made a defensive alliance, and it seemed that the two cities might live at peace.

This, however, was not to be, thanks to party changes in both cities and especially to the emergence of the Athenian Alcibiades, who intrigued with Argos. In 416 a great blot disfigured the pages of Athenian history when Melos, which revolted, was reduced, the men massacred and the women enslaved. In 415 it was decided to send a great expedition against Syracuse in the West, but through a series of mishaps this ended in total disaster for the Athenians. The attempt to besiege the city failed; the fleet was defeated in the Great Harbour of Syracuse; and the army, thus isolated in the island, retreated inland but was overwhelmed: at least 200 ships and 4,000 hoplites were lost. Some revolts followed in the Athenian empire, and the Spartans made an agreement with the Persians, from whom they got money to build up the Peloponnesian fleet. These disasters to Athens, for which the democratic leaders were chiefly responsible, helped to undermine the internal stability of the state: in 411 B.C. the democracy succumbed to the rule of Four Hundred oligarchs. These were, however, replaced after a few months by a moderate democracy of 5,000. This the Athenian fleet at Samos refused to recognise, and full democracy was soon restored. Meantime the war was being fought by sea in the Aegean with varying fortune until in 405 the Athenian navy was finally annihilated at Aegospotami. Nearly all the allies revolted; Athens was besieged by land and sea, and surrendered in 404. The Athenians had to destroy their fortifications, surrender their fleet, give up all foreign possessions, and become subject allies of Sparta. This did not complete their suffering: thirty oligarchs seized power, and massacred their political opponents. By 403, however, they had been overthrown, civil war was ended, and democracy was restored.

Sparta thus stepped into the shoes of Athens and took over the old Athenian empire, which for the next few years it administered with considerable harshness, becoming involved in the process with its former ally, Persia, for whose throne Prince Cyrus had made an unsuccessful bid. Cyrus' career ended at the battle of Cunaxa, after which the Ten Thousand Greek mercenaries who had helped him had to fight their way back to Greece from the heart of Asia under the leadership of Xenophon. But Sparta's overseas empire was lost when the Persians defeated the Peloponnesian fleet off Cnidus in 394. In Greece an anti-Spartan coalition grew up, and it was joined by Athens, which was gradually regaining strength. This so-called Corinthian War dragged on until 386 when it was brought to an end through Persian mediation, although at the cost of sacrificing the Asiatic Greeks to Persia. Under the leadership of King Agesilaus Sparta followed an oppressive policy towards its neighbours, which culminated in a treacherous attack on Thebes, where the Spartans seized the citadel (382). This stirred up the forces of freedom, and in 379/8 Thebes was liberated and gradually regained control of Boeotia. Athens formed an anti-Spartan League to fight by sea (377), but in creating this new confederacy carefully avoided some of the mistakes made in the first. Thus by 371 Sparta was ready for peace, but while it was being arranged Thebes broke off negotiations: a great battle between Sparta and Thebes followed at Leuctra, and for once Sparta was defeated. The thirty years of its hegemony in Greece were ended, and the Peloponnesian League dissolved. To protect themselves the cities of Arcadia formed a League and asked Thebes for help. Led by Epaminondas, a Theban army invaded Laconia and Messenia in 369 and freed the Messenians. Sparta thus lost half its territory and over half its serfs; it never regained its former strength.

Thus for a decade Thebes became the leading power in Greece, but failed to improve upon the methods of Athens or Sparta in exercising power. In the end a battle at Mantinea in 362, though a Theban victory, showed that Thebes' aim of hegemony in the Peloponnese was unattainable. It was indeed becoming clear to many that the idea of the self-sufficient and completely independent city-state might have to give place to other forms: otherwise history would continue as a series of attempts by one such city to dominate the rest. One result was to force those who felt themselves threatened to unite in leagues, and there were some interesting but not altogether successful attempts at federation during the fourth century, as in Chalcidice, Boeotia, Arcadia, Thessaly, and the Second Athenian League. But in fact unity was to be imposed on Greece from outside, from Macedon.

The Peloponnesian War had exerted great strains upon traditional ways of thought in religion and ethics at Athens, not least in the naked appeal to ruthless power politics that some leaders had made. These tendencies were reinforced by the Sophists. Many were men of wide knowledge, but the teaching of some challenged accepted beliefs. For instance, Thrasymachus argued that 'justice is the interest of the stronger', while a fresh emphasis on the individual affected the normal relation of citizen and

Theatre masks for (left to right) comic, satyric, and tragic actors.

state. The greatest of these teachers was Socrates. Although a most loyal citizen of Athens, he set an even greater value on intellectual freedom and the inner voice of God. Thus when in 399 he was accused of impiety, he preferred death to compromise. On the stage also traditional views were challenged by Euripides (ca. 485–406), who was critical of the wisdom of the Homeric gods and portrayed the passions and feelings of ordinary men and women with realism and psychological understanding. A belief in the older values was expressed in comedies by Aristophanes (ca. 450–385), behind whose gaiety, vitality, and humour lay a serious strain. A passionate lover of Athens, he did not hesitate to ridicule its weaknesses and to attack in scurrilous terms the politicians of whom he disapproved. That this could be done on the open stage and in wartime, when most governments tighten censorship, is a measure of the freedom of speech that Athens enjoyed. Although no pacifist, Aristophanes yearned for peace and an end to the war that had ravaged Greece so long. The disruptive effects of war on standards of human conduct were analysed with terrifying clarity and penetration by Thucydides in his *History of the Peloponnesian War*. He himself served in it until he was exiled in 424 for having failed to save Amphipolis when he was in command in this area. More critical and 'scientific' in his historical method than Herodotus, he produced a work of unsurpassed ability. It is true that he is analysing small city-states at war; but his profound knowledge of human nature and human motives, which do not change fundamentally from one century to another, has made his study a 'classic' of permanent value to all concerned with man's conduct of war or politics. At the time that Thucydides was diagnosing the human mind in the individual and society, a doctor, Hippocrates of Cos (ca. 460–400), was advancing the study of the human body by detailed observation and not least by a rational approach to disease that shook itself free from all superstitious or religious taboos. Yet despite the rationalism of the Periclean age and the teaching of the Sophists, despite the weakening of the simple religious beliefs of the family, much superstition lingered on and oracle-mongers flourished: the statesman Nicias, in command of the expedition against Syracuse, was swayed by oracles and omens, and Cleon and Alcibiades exploited such beliefs for political ends.

THE RISE OF MACEDON AND
ALEXANDER THE GREAT

Macedon was somewhat cut off from the Greek world: in the south it was blocked by Thessaly and by coastal cities many of which were allies of Athens; on the west was a barrier of mountains; and in the north and west barbarian Illyrians and Paeonians pressed on the frontiers. The population was mixed: Illyrian and Thracian elements were mingled with the incoming Dorians. During the fifth century the country became Hellenised, more united, and stronger. This process was accelerated by Philip, who seized royal power in 359 B.C. and defeated the Illyrians. The Macedonians were bound closely to their kings by ties of personal service in war and peace, and Philip secured the devotion of the Macedonian army at a time when most Greek states were relying more upon mercenaries than citizens. He improved his army by reforms that included the development of the phalanx of infantry armed with long spears (*sarissae*). Before long he occupied Amphipolis, Pydna (357), and Potidaea (356), and then founded a city, Philippi, which gave him control of the gold mines of Mount Pangaeus. This expansion provoked the hostility of the Athenians, but their attention was distracted by a revolt of their allies (the Social War) that had been encouraged by Mausolus of Caria. This monarch, who had moved his capital to Halicarnassus, was turning his country into a great sea power; but it failed to grow into a permanent challenge to Athens. In fact the most lasting mark of his rule was his monumental tomb or Mausoleum which was regarded as one of the seven wonders of the world.

Meantime Philip during the next ten years (356–346), by intrigue and calculated intervention in Greek quarrels became the dominant power in the Greek world. The Athenians, who had made peace with him in 346, were divided in their attitude: was he sincere in his peaceful declarations to Athens, or was he planning further aggression? While Aeschines urged that he should be trusted, Demosthenes tried to awaken his fellow-citizens to a realisation of their perils in a series of public speeches that included the *Philippics*. When Philip, who had turned Thrace into a province in 342–341, besieged Byzantium in 340, Athens declared war. In 338, at the invitation of the Delphic Amphictiony, Philip invaded Greece. Thanks to Demosthenes' efforts, Thebes was persuaded to join Athens in resisting the invader. The rival armies met at Chaeronea in 338, and Philip was victorious. He punished Thebes severely but was lenient to Athens. He turned his victory to wise use. Since the Greek city-states had failed to unite, he determined to impose unity upon them. He proclaimed

The cities played a dominant rôle in the history of Greece. **90.** Sparta, an example of a district isolated by high mountains. **91.** Corinth owed its importance as a trade centre to its favourable situation on the isthmus between Attica and the Peloponnese. In the centre, the old town; in the background, one of the two harbours between which Corinth lay. **92.** Little of Thebes has survived; the former agora is now a cornfield. **93.** Argos, at the foot of a hill, dominated the Argive plain. **94.** Strong walls surrounded many cities. The 4th cent. remains of Aegosthena at the E. extremity of the Gulf of Corinth give some idea of former defence works. **95.** Ruined walls of Paestum in S. Italy. **96.** Foundations still show the course of the former circular wall of the city of Mantinea in the heart of the Peloponnese.

90

91

92

93

95

96

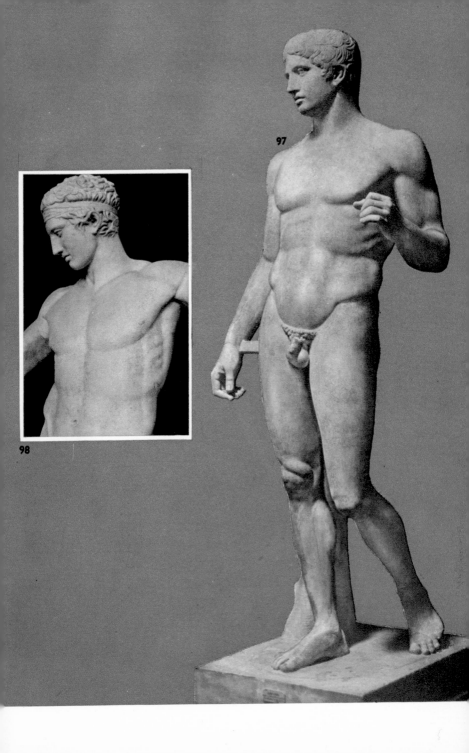

97

98

99

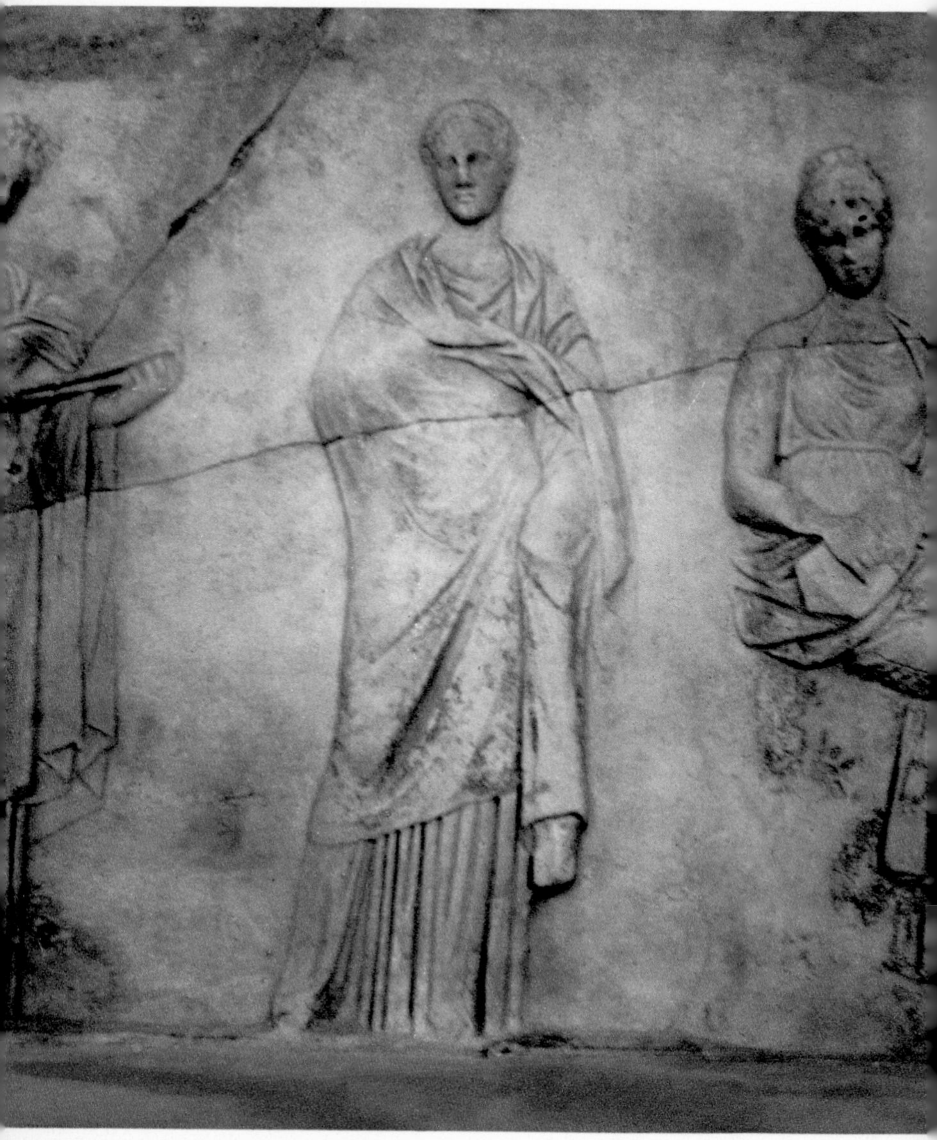

100

101

102

a general peace and established a General Assembly of the Greeks; this Hellenic League formed an alliance with Macedon. Philip then planned to realise ideas that the Athenian Isocrates had long been advocating, namely that a united Greece should take the offensive against the old national enemy, Persia. But when, as Leader (*hegemon*), he was about to lead the forces of Greece and Macedon to free the Asiatic Greeks from Persian rule, he was murdered (336).

Philip's plans were carried out by his son Alexander, who at the age of twenty was proclaimed king by the assembly of the Macedonian army. His tutor, Aristotle, had encouraged his deep appreciation of Greek culture, and Alexander had already shown great powers of intellect and leadership. Having made sure that Greece would remain loyal in his absence, in 334 he crossed the Hellespont with some 40,000 men. He defeated the Persian army at the river Granicus and then freed the Greek cities in Asia Minor. He disbanded his fleet and then defeated Darius and the Persian army at Issus (333). After reducing Tyre by siege (a most difficult operation), he rejected Darius' offer to surrender all territory west of the Euphrates: clearly he had resolved to destroy the Persian Empire. But first he went to Egypt, where as the successor of the Pharaohs he received divine honours, and where he founded the first and greatest of the cities named Alexandria. In 331 he defeated at Gaugamela in Mesopotamia the fresh army that Darius had raised. He then occupied Babylon, sacked Persepolis, and overran all Persia. He next pursued Darius, who had fled from Gaugamela, but when he reached the Caspian Gates he found the king dead. He now assumed the title of king and prepared to occupy the eastern part of his empire, although his Greek and Macedonian followers were ready to regard the war as over; further, he began to wear Persian dress and to draft Persian troops into his army. Then followed his spectacular triumphs in the East:

Greek art reached its zenith in the 5th and 4th centuries B.C. Some works by the great masters are still known from originals or copies. One of the first to employ exact calculations in representing the human body was Polyclitus of Argos. The lance-bearer (**97**) and statue of a young man (**98**) are both by his hand. **99**. Fragment of a relief, representing Leto and two Muses. **101**. Head by Scopas, from the temple of Athena Alea at Tegea. **102**. Bronze head of a boxer, attributed to Silanion. **100**. The skill of Greek painters can be seen from vase-paintings: detail of a work by Meidias, dating from the time of the Peloponnesian War and representing the Rape of the daughters of Leucippus. **103**. This Attic tombstone, on which Hegeso examines jewels handed to her by a servant, dates from ca. 400 B.C.; it is highly typical of the depth and beauty of classical relief sculpture.

he conquered Bactria and Sogdiana (Afghanistan and Turkestan), marrying a Sogdian wife, Roxane (330–329), and then overran northwest India (327–325). His return journey was a voyage of discovery down the Indus and on through the desert of Gedrosia (Baluchistan). By 324 he was back in Susa. Though he had meantime met with considerable opposition from some of his Greek followers, he tried to weld all his peoples together: eighty of his officers married Iranians (he himself married as his second wife a daughter of Darius), and at Opis on the Tigris he held a great feast of reconciliation and unity. But at Babylon in 323 he caught a fever and died at the age of thirty-two.

A brief account of his conquests can give little impression of the magnitude of his achievements or of the driving force and genius of the man who planned and executed them. The problems of administration and finance were immense, but they were helped by his policy of founding new cities, of which some twenty-five are known. These were designed not only to Hellenise the East but also to stimulate a greater fusion of East and West. It is no exaggeration to say that this young man, who appeared as a hero out of his favourite book, the *Iliad*, changed the whole course of ancient history. Not only did he free the Asiatic Greeks, but he opened up the vast Persian Empire, with all its wealth and natural resources, to a Greece that urgently needed the opportunity for economic expansion, and at the same time he promoted the spread of Greek culture and weakened national barriers. Not least, he showed that the day of the city-state in the old sense was over: the future lay with monarchy and large territorial states.

Meantime the Greek cities in the West had been pursuing their own lives. With the death of Hieron of Syracuse in 466 not only did tyranny end for some time but Sicilian culture declined from its earlier glories. Syracuse, which had repelled the Athenian attack in 413, was exhausted, and was thus exposed to renewed pressure from the Carthaginians, who overran much of the island. The Carthaginian menace was resisted only at the price of renewed tyranny. At Syracuse Dionysius I gained power in 405, dominated eastern Sicily, and constructed a state that included part of southern Italy. Thus at the cost of their individual liberties the Greek cities were enabled to drive back the Carthaginians; but the new state did not survive the death in 366 of its creator and master. His son Dionysius II was a weaker man, and all the efforts of Plato and Dion failed to turn him into an ideal philosopher-king. In 345 he was driven out with the help of the Corinthian general Timoleon, who managed to remove the lesser tyrants in other Sicilian cities. But before long the restored free governments again began to lose ground: Syracuse, for example, had by 317 once more succumbed to a tyrant, this time Agathocles.

The intellectual and artistic achievements of the fourth century were remarkable. In literature it was an age of prose rather than of poetry. Tragedy declined after Euripides, but comedy, although losing the full-blooded vigour of Aristophanes and his contemporaries, was still written and acted by the poets of the so-called Middle Comedy period (ca. 400–320), when it became less political and more concerned with daily life and manners. In the field of historical writing the chief names are Xenophon, Ephorus, and Theopompus. But the fourth century was above all the age of oratory and philosophy, which reflected its emphasis on the individual. In the law-courts and Assembly the art of oratory was brought to great heights by men like Lysias, Isaeus, Isocrates, Aeschines, and Demosthenes. Following in the tradition of the Sophists, Isocrates developed higher education at Athens in what was equivalent to a university, while in 387 the Academy was established by Socrates' great disciple, Plato (ca. 429–347). It is impossible here to indicate the range of his philosophical thought or his theory of knowledge. He wished to apply the result of his intellectual inquiry to the life of the individual and the community. Thus in the

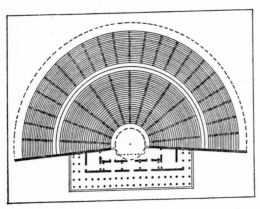

Plan of the theatre at Epidaurus (see also Plate 80).

Republic he was concerned with the nature of justice, and also with its practical application: what was the ideal state and what type of education would produce it? In the *Laws* he worked out his ideas in much more detail. Plato's greatest pupil at the Academy was Aristotle from Stagirus (ca. 385–322), who in 335 started another philosophical centre at the Lyceum. Like Plato, he was concerned with the nature of the state, and still continued to think in terms of the small city-state. In addition to writing the *Politics*, in which he developed political theory, he described 158 Greek constitutions; of these only *The Constitution of Athens* survives. Aristotle's interests were encyclopaedic; besides politics he wrote on ethics, rhetoric, and poetry, while his orderly mind found satisfaction in close observation and the classification of the animal world. Others made advances in mathematics, mechanics, and geographical studies. Some philosophers reacted against normal city life: Diogenes, for example, lived in a barrel. He was named the Dog and his followers were called Cynics; they believed that self-mastery led to self-sufficiency and so to happiness.

Artistic developments in the fourth century laid more stress on naturalism and individualism. Great sculptors like Praxiteles of Athens emphasised the human rather than the divine aspects of deities, as seen in his statue of Hermes with the child Dionysus. Scopas of Paros emphasised strong emotions, while Lysippus of Sicyon was famed for his battle scenes and portraiture. In painting Apelles followed similar traditions, excelling in portraits and realistic figures. Fine buildings continued to adorn the cities of Greece and the East, such as the Mausoleum at Halicarnassus and the temple of Artemis at Ephesus. In Greece the theatre at Epidaurus still survives to evoke admiration.

Such artistic and intellectual achievement presupposes fairly stable economic and social conditions. The wars of the fourth century, following close on the Peloponnesian War, involved much loss of life and property. Where agriculture suffered, some cities, such as Athens, were able to develop their industries; cities increased in size, labour in some factories became more specialised, and banking and commercial speculation increased. But although wages rose, they failed to keep up with the cost of living, and the opening up of the East by Alexander's conquests came just in time to redress the balance and to establish the basis for the prosperity of the Hellenistic world.

THE HELLENISTIC WORLD

At Alexander's death his vast empire tended to fall apart. His generals in rivalry with each other at first tried to gain control of the whole; but after a long series of wars they realised that each must be content with what he could seize and hold. By 275 B.C. three new dynastic kingdoms had been established, that of the Ptolemies in Egypt and southern Syria, that of the Seleucids in Asia from the Aegean to the Hindu Kush, with its heart in Syria, and that of the Antigonids in Macedonia and part of Greece (e.g. Corinth). Of the long struggles for power between these three monarchies, until at length they were all dominated by Rome, little can be said here. It will be more profitable to glance at some of the more positive achievements in this Hellenistic world, which was united by a common civilisation and a common speech, the widespread form of Greek that was known as the *Koinē*.

The Syrian kingdom was founded by Alexander's general Seleucus. He and his son Antiochus I followed the example of Alexander as a founder of cities: in order to strengthen and control their empire they established a great number of Greek cities and military colonies in Asia Minor, Syria (e.g. Antioch), and Babylonia (e.g. Seleucia on the Tigris). Later two separate kingdoms split off. Pergamum gradually threw off Seleucid control, and under the Attalid dynasty it remained independent from about 263 to 133 B.C.; and Euthydemus (ca. 208) won Bactria and his son built up the kingdom to include northwestern India. But these Greek principalities in the Indus valley were overwhelmed by the first century B.C.

In Egypt Alexander's general, Ptolemy I, become the successor of the Pharaohs. With his capital at Alexandria, he was not only king but the embodiment of the state that he owned. He controlled the whole economic system, since the land was his. Production and manufactures were state monopolies, and in order that all the royal dues should be collected, a vast bureaucracy gradually grew up which got a stranglehold on the country and led to much corruption, oppression, and unrest. The result, however, of this economic planning was to increase the wealth of the country, and particularly of the Ptolemies and their Greek officials. This was reflected in the growth of Alexandria, which became the largest Greek city in the world; with its harbours and lighthouse, it was a great commercial centre, while Ptolemy I had founded there a huge Library and Museum, so that it was also a centre of culture and research.

Macedon passed to the control of various overlords until Antigonus Gonatas (276–241) established a more stable rule. He protected the country from barbarian attack (Celts had ravaged Greece in 279), and as a friend of Zeno, the founder of Stoicism, he claimed to rule as the servant of his people. In 262 he took Athens, which for some time had been independent and had opposed him in the Chremonidean War (267–262). Though Athens recovered freedom in 229, it had become little more than a university town. Other Greek cities had tried to maintain their freedom by combining into leagues. Most of the Peloponnese had combined with Corinth in the Achaean League, while much of northern Greece had formed an Aetolian League, in which there was virtually a common citizenship for members of the nearer states and isopolity (potential citizenship) for those farther afield. In Greece states tried to avoid mutual warfare by more frequent recourse to arbitration, and the upper classes were prosperous, though the plight of the poor became worse and very occasionally (e.g. at Sparta under Cleomenes III in 226) it found expression in social revolution. Finally, no account of the Hellenistic world would be complete without a reference to the island republic of Rhodes, the Venice of the ancient world, which became a flourishing commercial state, whose trade was guarded by an efficient navy.

Thus most of the cities of the Greek homeland managed to avoid monarchy and retain republican government, albeit often limited by federal obligations or the long arm of Macedon. But a large part of the Greek world fell under the domination of one or other of the three great monarchs. Within these monarchies individual cities might keep a large measure of local autonomy, but they were subject to the overriding authority of the king. These monarchs were absolute; but they were Greeks and did not fully imitate the traditions of Eastern absolute monarchy. Thus they lived in relative simplicity of outward style, and so far from seeking Oriental seclusion they often took an active personal share in administration in peace and war. But gradually there was a move to deify these living rulers in Egypt and Syria. As gods these usurpers would have a justification for their power, while to the common man they were the Benefactors, the givers of all the prosperity that he enjoyed. Ptolemy I had assumed the divine honours of the native Pharaohs, valid in the eyes of his native subjects; but in 271 a Greek cult was established for the reigning Ptolemy. This practice was followed by the Seleucids, but not in Macedon, where not even the dead kings were worshipped.

In this new world, where Greek settlers penetrated in large numbers into Eastern areas, Greeks and Orientals mingled to a considerable extent, since the Greeks had little prejudice in matters of race or colour: it was rather culture that separated Greeks from 'barbarians'. This belief in their superior culture, however, led them to retain for themselves a higher political status than the Orientals: government and administration remained essentially in their hands. But the creation of these large political units stimulated and facilitated trade and industry, while the quest for wealth encouraged exploration. More was learnt about India, the Caspian, and the Red Sea; Pytheas of Marseilles discovered the 'Pretannic Islands', Albion and Ierne (Britain and Ireland), and reached 'Thule' (?Norway).

The Hellenistic rulers and their wealthy citizens were natural patrons of art. Architecture received great stimulus from the founding of numerous new cities as well as from fresh building in old. Regular rectangular town-planning became normal, and since the spirit of the age was more secular than religious, new temples were less conspicuous than palaces, theatres, gymnasia, and colonnades. Cities, of which Alexandria and Pergamum are examples, were magnificently laid out and adorned. Sculpture was helped by the practice of erecting public memorial statues. Many fine works were produced, such as the Winged Victory of Samothrace, the Melian Aphrodite, the 'Dying Gladiator', and the 'Wrestlers', while the tendency to exaggeration and strain is seen in the battle of the gods and giants depicted in the frieze of the great altar at Pergamum. Portraiture was excellent, both in sculpture and on the coins. Hellenistic influences increased in the East and exerted a strong influence on Buddhist art.

The production of literature was prolific and was encouraged by royal patronage, not least that of the Ptolemies at the Museum of Alexandria. The reading public increased, and its spread was helped by the Koinē. Poetry is represented by the pastoral idylls of Theocritus, the epic *Argonautica* of Apollonius Rhodius, the varied poetry of Callimachus, Cleanthes' Hymn to Zeus, and the New Comedy at Athens, of which Menander was one of the brightest stars. Historical writing included a history of Alexander by Ptolemy I and the history of some of the Diadochi (Successors) by Hieronymus of Cardia. Histories of Athens were written by Philochorus (ca. 275), and other local histories, biographies, and memoirs appeared. At Alexandria and elsewhere men studied language and grammar, and scholars tried to establish accurate texts of earlier authors such as Homer. Studies were pursued in many branches of knowledge. As Aristotle had laid the foundations of zoology, so his pupil Theophrastus applied his methods to botany. Discoveries in medicine and anatomy, through dissection, led to striking developments in surgery, and the relation of nerves to brain was discovered. Great strides were made in mathematics. Euclid's work in geometry became a textbook that lasted for over 2,000 years, while the achievements of Archimedes were manifold in mechanics and hydrostatics as well as in pure mathematics. Indeed with the invention of a steam-engine the Hellenistic world was on the edge of a mechaniical revolution. In astronomy Aristarchus of Samos thought that the earth went round the sun, but his view did not displace the geocentric theory which held the field until the time of Copernicus. Eratosthenes (ca. 225) was the creator of scientific geography and estimated the circumference of the earth to within 200 miles of the correct figure. Thus the Hellenistic world made a spectacular contribution to natural science; that it did not do even more was due partly to the lack of precision instruments and partly to the gradual decline in spirit in a world where magic and astrology began to revive under the stress of misfortune.

In philosophy two main currents of belief emerged. Epicurus (ca. 342–271) took up the atomic theories of Democritus (p. 40) and held an essentially materialist view of life: its aim was pleasure, though primarily intellectual pleasure, and this must be sought by freedom from desire and worry and by a withdrawal from public life. By contrast Zeno, the founder of the Stoics —so-called because he used to teach in a porch (*stoa*) in Athens—taught that happiness was attained by living in harmony with nature: by a self-sufficient disregard of external circumstances and by withdrawing into his own soul a man could become master of his fate. Man must freely bend his own will to the divine will. Further, the universe was a cosmopolitan society of men and gods, in which all men were equal. Stoicism made a wide appeal, especially when later teachers had modified some of the harsher aspects of the earlier doctrine. For those whom philosophy did not attract, there were increasing numbers of Eastern religions coming into the Greek world (for example those of Isis and Syrian deities), while ideas of Fortune or Fate weighed heavily on the minds of many. Some sought relief in astrology, others in the Mystery religions. The world of the city-state, with its own deities and beliefs, was gone, and men found themselves in a wider, but in some respects a more alarming world.

Developments after Alexander the Great enabled Greek culture to spread over the known world. Macedonian control of Greece had been gained by the battle of Chaeronea; from an ancient monument a lion gazes over the battlefield (104). 105. Alexander. 106. Temple of Apollo at Didyma. 107. Alongside Hellenistic 'baroque', earlier forms continued, but with their vigour diminished: Doric-style temple at Nemea. 108. Alexander as the deified son of Ammon. Two of Alexander's successors: Seleucus I of Syria (109), and Ptolemy I of Egypt (110), with reverse (111). 112. Hellenism influenced local art forms: Gandhara (India) sculptures have been referred to as Graeco-Buddhist art. 113. Alexandria, a great Hellenistic city; the white lines indicate the street plan of the ancient city. 114. Tyre, built on an island; to capture it, Alexander constructed a causeway linking it to the mainland.

104

105

108

109

110

111

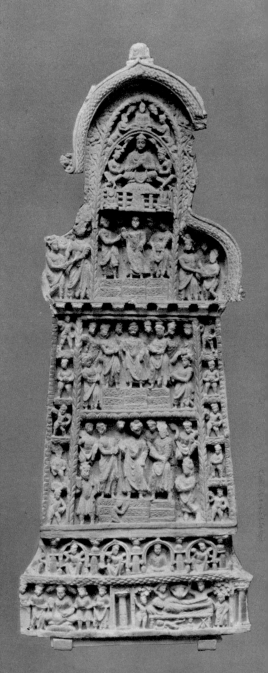

112

113

114

116

117

119

EARLY ITALY

When the Romans became the dominant power in Italy, the population of the peninsula was much mixed as the result of a long period of settlement by early peoples and tribes. The form this settlement had taken was largely influenced by geographical conditions (see p. 12). The primitive settlements of Neolithic man were gradually superseded by those of Indo-European peoples who brought with them the use of bronze. During the second millennium B.C. much of Italy was inhabited by peoples whose culture has been named by archaeologists the 'Apennine culture', while in the plains north of the Apennines other Bronze Age peoples, who had probably come from over the Alps, protected themselves in the swamps of the Po valley by constructing their villages on platforms supported on piles. These latter peoples practised agriculture and cremated their dead, whereas the Apennine folk practised burial. Soon after 1000 B.C. much of central Italy, as far south as Rome, was overrun by another Indo-European people, whom modern archaeologists have called Villanovans, after a typical settlement at Villanova near Bologna. They brought with them (from central Europe?) the use of iron. The peoples on the east coast of Italy (for example in Picenum and Apulia) were subjected to strong Illyrian influences from across the Adriatic. When all these early Indo-European peoples had found homes for themselves and settled down, two main groups can be distinguished: the Latins who thrust into the coastal plain later named Latium, and the tribes who spoke kindred Umbro–Sabellian dialects and remained in the highlands of central Italy.

Before long we find that much of the area occupied by the Villanovans is in the hands of the Etruscans. The problem of the origin of the Etruscans

Although the great paintings of this era have disappeared, painted vases and the wall-paintings that have survived at places such as Pompeii and Herculaneum give some idea of this branch of Hellenistic art. **115.** An important work from Herculaneum is The Feeding of Telephus by a Hind. **116.** One feature of Hellenistic art is its monumentality. This is very prominent at Pergamum, centre of an art form which, despite its inflated style, attained a striking virtuosity. An altar dedicated to Zeus there displays the colossal nature of this art. **117.** Genre sculpture was another feature of the period: bronze statue of a jockey. Another example of the often dramatic art of Pergamum is The Dying Gaul, marble copy of a bronze original. **119.** The history of Rome may be introduced with a relief of the goddess Roma amidst horses and lictors in a triumphal procession.

still remains unsolved. Possibly their civilisation developed out of the amalgam of local peoples under the stimulus of influences from the East, but more probably Herodotus was right when he said that the Etruscans themselves had come from Asia Minor. One of the strongest arguments in support of this view is that their language, which has been only very partially deciphered, is certainly not an Indo-European tongue. They were probably a sea-faring people who descended on the coast of Etruria, attracted in part by its mineral resources, the copper of Etruria and the iron of Elba, and they created in Italy a much more advanced civilisation than had existed there hitherto. They established themselves as a conquering aristocracy in a number of fortified self-governing cities which were first ruled by kings such as Lars Porsenna of Clusium and later by nobles.

The profits of war, trade, industry, and agriculture enriched the Etruscan overlords, who became a ruling caste of feudal barons and enjoyed a luxurious life. The frescoes of their tombs and the magnificent gold-work and jewellery found in them show how they indulged in feasting and banquets, in dancing and music, in sports and horse-racing. Under their stimulus the artistic products of Greece and the Orient flowed into Etruria (ca. 750–600 B.C.) and inspired native craftsmen. The Etruscans were great builders and engineers: they cleared the forests, drained the land, and built strong cities adorned with temples. Their religious ritual was much concerned with divination and with death; there was a strong streak of cruelty in their nature, as seen in their delight in gladiatorial combats. From Etruria their power radiated outwards, southwards as far as Campania and northwards over the Apennines, while their strength at sea was considerable. Thus in alliance with the Carthaginians they defeated the Phocaeans in 535 in a naval action off Alalia in Corsica, which had been founded by the Phocaeans about 560. But while at this time it looked as if they might soon succeed in uniting the whole of Italy, in fact the tide rapidly turned against them. After being defeated by the Greeks of Cumae in Campania in 524, they were soon forced out of Latium and back to the north of the Tiber, and then in 474 their navy was defeated by Hieron of Syracuse. Thus their power was gradually confined to the district that still bears their name, Tuscany, and their artistic achievements began to decline.

A second people who played a major rôle in civilising Italy were those Greek colonists who, as already seen (p. 27), settled in large numbers around the toe and heel of Italy. They may have been preceded by their Mycenaean ancestors in setting up small trading-posts, but the first full-scale settlement of Greeks started in the eighth century. One of the earliest colonies was at Cumae (ca. 740 B.C.), which became famed for the oracle of the Sibyl and the temple of Apollo. From these and other centres Greek influences spread through southern Italy, but they did not penetrate deeply north of Campania: Magna Graecia remained part of the Mediterranean world and very largely turned its back upon central Italy.

Considerably later another people began to affect the history of Italy. During the fourth century marauding groups of Celts migrated from their great empire in central Europe and began to overrun the northern plain of Italy, from which they finally ousted the Etruscans. Thus the area became known to the Romans as Cisalpine Gaul. In some respects these Celtic tribes had reached a high standard of culture, but in others they remained wild savages.

Thus in early Italy there was a very great variety of peoples, languages, cultures, and traditions. The great question was whether some order and unity might emerge, and all these peoples be fused into one nation, or whether they would continue, like the Greeks, as small entities often at war with one another. The solution of this problem, which defeated the Etruscans, was reserved for the political skill of the Roman people.

EARLY ROME

The Latin-speaking peoples who occupied the area known later as Latium were akin, at any rate in part, to the Villanovans. They built their villages on the hills that rose from the plain. One of these shepherds' settlements grew up on the hills near a ford across the river Tiber, some fifteen miles from its mouth. The earliest settlers on this site of the later city of Rome occupied the Palatine hill, where traces of their Iron Age huts still survive. They deposited the ashes of their dead, whom they cremated, in the marshy ground below, where later the Forum developed. Settlers (Sabines?) on neighbouring hills buried their dead in the same spot. Gradually these small villages began to co-operate and to coalesce into a single settlement under the leadership of a single king. Tradition records seven kings of early Rome; the founder Romulus may be dismissed as a legend, but not most of the rest. The fifth king was called Tarquin, an Etruscan name, and it is clear that Rome was engulfed in the southward expansion of the Etruscans and had to submit to their domination, which lasted through most of the sixth century. But this period of Etruscan rule was not an unmitigated misfortune for the early Romans, since they were introduced to a higher level of civilisation. Rome now became a city in the Greek sense of the word. It was protected by earth-works, if not by a continuous stone wall, the Forum area was drained, and many buildings and temples were constructed, including the great temple on the Capitoline hill later dedicated to Jupiter Optimus Maximus. In art, religion, and culture the Etruscans taught the Romans much, but they did not impose their language, and when the Etruscan dynasty was ejected Rome was still essentially a Latin city. But during this period the Romans had been swept into a wider world of industry and commerce, and had at the same time extended their influence in Latium, gaining control of some 350 square miles of territory.

In 510 B.C. Tarquinius Superbus was expelled from Rome, and with this both Etruscan domination and the monarchy came to an end at Rome. The story of his fall is embellished in Roman tradition with many a legend, such as the story of Lucretia; but in fact it fits into the wider picture of the general collapse of Etruscan power south of Latium. The Greeks in Campania and now the Latins were moving to the offensive and asserting their independence. Having got rid of a foreign king, the Romans decided that they had finished with monarchy and in its place they established a Republic. This was to be administered by two magistrates (consuls), who were to be elected each year and to have equal authority. In other words, the executive authority (*imperium*), which the king had wielded for life, was divided between two men who would hold it for one year only. The general direction of public affairs fell to the leaders of the noble clans (*gentes*), who met in an assembly, the Senate. Previously they had advised the king; now they would advise the magistrates and deliberate on the needs of the *respublica* on traditional lines, following custom (*mos maiorum*). The people as a whole, the *populus Romanus*, met in an assembly (*Comitia*) to vote on matters put before them by the magistrates; but the voting system gave the rich greater influence than the poor. For military purposes the people had been divided up into five classes in accordance with the amount of their property, and also into smaller groups of a hundred (*centuriae*). The members of these

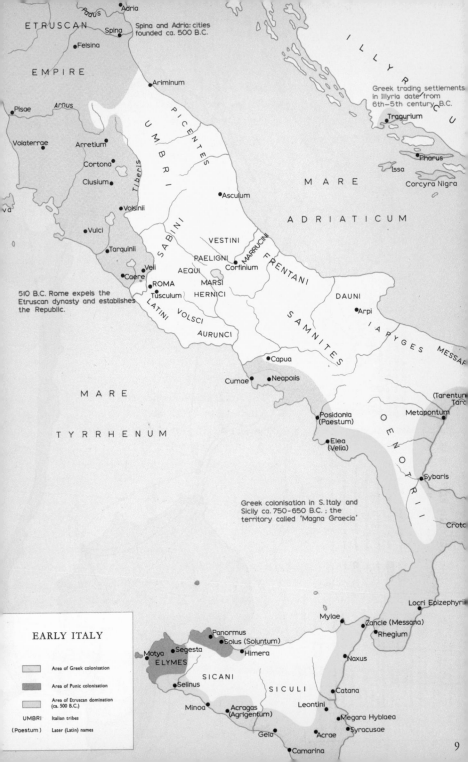

ETRUSCAN

Padus
● Adria

Spina
● Felsina

Spina and Adria: cities
founded ca. 500 B.C.

EMPIRE

ILLYRICU

● Ariminum

● Pisae

Arnus

UMBRI

PICENTES

Greek trading settlements
in Illyria date from
6th–5th century B.C.

● Tragurium

Volaterrae

Arretium ●

Tiberis

● Pharus

Cortona ●

Issa

Clusium ●

● Asculum

MARE

Corcyra Nigra

● Volsinii

SABINI

VESTINI

ADRIATICUM

● Vulci

● Tarquinii

PAELIGNI

MARRUCINI

FRENTANI

● Veii

AEQUI

Corfinium ●

Caere ●

● ROMA

MARSI

510 B.C. Rome expels the
Etruscan dynasty and establishes
the Republic.

Tusculum ●

HERNICI

DAUNI

LATINI

VOLSCI

● Arpi

AURUNCI

SAMNITES

IAPYGES

MESSAP

● Capua

Cumae ●

● Neapolis

(Tarentum
Tarc

MARE

● Posidonia
(Paestum)

Metapontum ●

TYRRHENUM

● Elea
(Velia)

OENOTRII

● Sybaris

Greek colonisation in S. Italy and
Sicily ca. 750–650 B.C.; the
territory called 'Magna Graecia'

● Croto

● Locri Epizephyrii

● Mylae

Zancle (Messana) ●

Panormus ●

● Rhegium

Solus (Soluntum) ●

Motya ●

Segesta ●

● Himera

ELYMES

● Naxus

SICANI

Selinus ●

SICULI

● Catana

● Minoa

Acragas
(Agrigentum) ●

Leontini ●

● Megara Hyblaea

● Acrae

Syracusae ●

Gela ●

● Camarina

EARLY ITALY

Area of Greek colonisation

Area of Punic colonisation

Area of Etruscan domination
(ca. 500 B.C.)

UMBRI   Italian tribes

(Paestum) Later (Latin) names

9

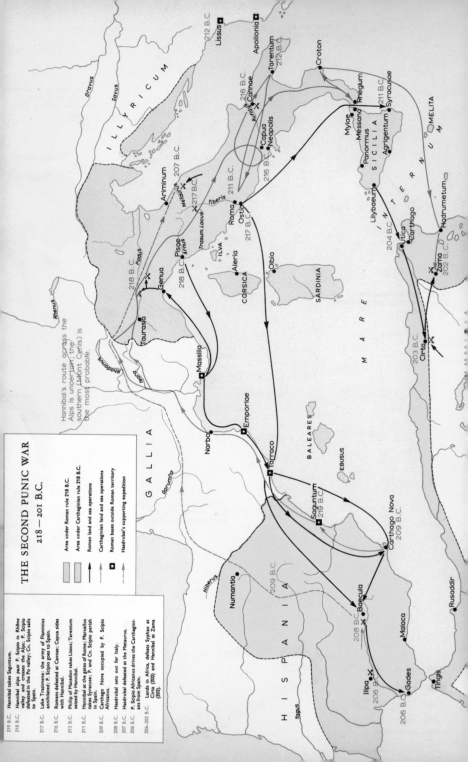

THE SECOND PUNIC WAR
218 — 201 B.C.

Area under Roman rule 218 B.C.

Area under Carthaginian rule 218 B.C.

→ Roman land and sea operations

→ Carthaginian land and sea operations

□ Roman bases outside Roman territory

⇢ Hasdrubal's supporting expedition

219 B.C.   Hannibal takes Saguntum.

218 B.C.   Hannibal slips past P. Scipio in Rhône valley and crosses the Alps; P. Scipio defeated in the Po valley; Cn. Scipio sails to Spain.

217 B.C.   Lake Trasimene; the army of Flaminius annihilated; P. Scipio goes to Spain.

216 B.C.   Roman defeated at Cannae; Capua sides with Hannibal.

213 B.C.   Philip of Macedon takes Lissus; Tarentum seized by Hannibal.

211 B.C.   Hannibal at the gates of Rome; Marcellus takes Syracuse; P. and Cn. Scipio perish in Spain.

209 B.C.   Carthago Nova occupied by P. Scipio Africanus.

208 B.C.   Hasdrubal sets out for Italy.

207 B.C.   Hasdrubal defeated at the Metaurus.

206 B.C.   P. Scipio Africanus drives the Carthaginians from Spain.

204–202 B.C.   Lands in Africa, defeats Syphax at Cirta (203) and Hannibal at Zama (202).

Hannibal's route across the Alps is uncertain; the southern route (Mont Cenis) is the most probable.

CAMPAIGNS OF GAIUS JULIUS CAESAR

100 B.C.   Caesar born at Rome.
61–60 B.C.   Campaign against the Lusitanians.
60 B.C.   Triumvirate of Caesar, Pompey, and Crassus
58–51 B.C.   Conquest of Gaul.
55–54 B.C.   Exploratory expeditions to Britain.
55–53 B.C.   Punitive expeditions against German tribes.
49 B.C.   Caesar crosses the Rubicon and marches against Pompey.
49 B.C.   Ilerda: Pompey's armies in Spain defeated.
48 B.C.   Caesar pursues Pompey and defeats him at Pharsalus.
47 B.C.   Caesar intervenes in the Egyptian war of succession; Alexandria occupied; Cleopatra placed on throne.
47 B.C.   Zela: Pompey's ally Pharnaces defeated; Caesar returns to Rome.
46 B.C.   Thapsus: Pompeian forces defeated.
45 B.C.   Munda: Pompeians defeated.
44 B.C.   Caesar murdered at Rome.

Territory under Roman rule in 100 B.C.
Areas conquered by Caesar
Extension of Roman power between 100 and 44 B.C. in which Caesar had no share
Caesar's campaigns in Spain and Gaul
Caesar's campaigns in the Civil War against Pompey

11

THE ROMAN EMPIRE IN THE TIME OF AUGUSTUS

44 B.C.   Caesar murdered; Octavian leaves Apollonia for Rome
43 B.C.   Triumvirate: Octavian, Antony, and Lepidus.
42 B.C.   Philippi: Octavian and Antony defeat Brutus and Cassius, Caesar's murderers.
31 B.C.   Actium: Octavian defeats his rival Antony and becomes sole ruler.
30 B.C.   Egypt incorporated in the Empire.
29–11 B.C.   Moesia conquered; not made a province until later.
27 B.C.   Numidia added to Africa.
27 B.C.   Crete and Cyrenaica united.
19 B.C.   Northwest corner of Spain pacified.
15 B.C.   Raetia and Noricum added to Empire as provinces.
12–7 B.C.   Expeditions under Drusus and Tiberius penetrate Germany as far as the Albis.
6 A.D.   Judaea made a province.
10 A.D.   Pannonia made a province.
14 A.D.   Death of Augustus

Roman Empire at the death of Augustus
Provincial boundaries in the reign of Augustus

12

THE ROMAN EMPIRE IN THE SECOND CENTURY A.D.

Legend:

Roman Empire in the 2nd century A.D.

- · - · - Provincial frontiers

Areas that were part of the Empire for relatively short periods

19 B.C. Year in which the territory became a province; for further details see inset

Inset (provincial notes):

- ACHAIA — Subjugated 146 B.C. detached from Macedonia 27 B.C.
- AFRICA — Annexed 146 B.C. Tripolis added ca. 105. Numidia formed Africa Nova, 46–27, then added to Africa Proconsularis.
- AGRI DECUMATES — Area held by Rome ca. A.D. 74–263.
- ARMENIA — Annexed and held A.D. 114–117
- BITHYNIA ET PONTUS — Bithynia a province from 74 B.C.; Pontus added 65 B.C. Pontus bequeathed to Rome 96 B.C.: province 74.
- CAPPADOCIA — Annexed A.D. 17; in 70 joined to Galatia until Trajan.
- DACIA — Province A.D. 106–ca. 275. Divided into two (Inferior and Superior) ca. 118 and into three (Porolissensis) before 133.
- GALATIA — Annexed 25 B.C.; extended 7 B.C.–A.D. 63 and 72, but reduced under Trajan and in 137.
- GALLIA — Narbonensis annexed ca. 121 B.C. Transalpina conquered by Caesar 58–50; divided into provinces by Augustus.
- GERMANIA — Two military districts along the Rhine from A.D. 17: re-organised into provinces by Domitian.
- HISPANIA — Two provinces (Citerior and Ulterior) 197 B.C. Under Augustus Citerior extended (as Tarraconensis) and Lusitania organised.
- ILLYRICUM — Dalmatia controlled by Rome since 167 B.C. Illyricum a province 27 B.C. Frontiers defined A.D. 10.
- JUDAEA — Controlled by Rome from 63 B.C. Roman province A.D. 6–41 and 44–70. Re-organised in 70; entitled Syria Palaestina in second century.
- MESOPOTAMIA — Annexed A.D. 115–117, and from ca. 165 and intermittently in third century.
- MOESIA — Conquered 29 B.C.: province A.D. 6: divided into two by Trajan.
- PANNONIA — Annexed 34 B.C. It included Judaea (63–40 B.C.). Commagene (A.D. 17–38 and after A.D. 72), and Damascus and Palmyra in A.D. 106. Divided into two in 198.
- SYRIA — Divided into two by Domitian.

centuries met for political as well as military purposes, and thus there developed an Assembly meeting by centuries (*Comitia Centuriata*), which amongst other things elected the consuls. As needs increased, the consuls had assistants, quaestors (who were later responsible mainly for financial matters), while at times of national emergency if the consuls reached a deadlock a solution might be found by appointing for a period of six months a dictator whose authority overrode that of the consuls.

A striking feature of Roman society was the part played by the family. The head of each family, the *paterfamilias*, had great authority over its members, and married women, *matronae*, were held in much respect. Further, society was divided into two classes, patricians and plebeians, a division which had arisen partly from economic pressures. The plebeians were Roman citizens, but they lacked many political, social, and economic privileges. They could vote, but they could not hold office or become senators; they could not intermarry with patricians; and they did not know the law or share in the state religion. The internal history of the first two centuries of the Republic is largely that of the Struggle of the Orders, the efforts made by the plebeians to win complete equality. The struggle also turned on economic questions: there was a shortage of land, and harsh debt laws caused many peasants to sink to a state of semi-serfdom. The problems were solved, partly by concessions wrung from the patricians, and partly through the expansion of Roman power in Italy and the consequent increase of Roman territory which was thus made available for distribution. The method used by the plebeians was to threaten to secede, to withdraw from Rome altogether, which the patricians could never allow, since only a united state could withstand the pressure of the external enemies by whom Rome was beset. Thus over the years the patricians had to concede one point after another. We cannot here enter into details, but may merely note a few landmarks and the fact that the constitution was hammered out in the course of this internal struggle.

Early in the fifth century the patricians were forced to recognise the existence of a purely plebeian assembly, the *Concilium Plebis*, which claimed to legislate for the whole community, a claim that was not fully conceded until 287 B.C. The plebeians also appointed their own officials to protect their interests against the arbitrary exercise of power by the patrician magistrates. These ten tribunes of the plebs gained increasing authority and influence. Further, the patricians were compelled to allow anyone condemned on a capital charge by a magistrate to appeal against the judgment to the people as a whole (*provocatio ad populum*), and in 450 B.C. they had to permit a commission to draw up and publish the law, the code of Twelve Tables, which became the fountainhead of Roman law. The plebeians now knew the law, although the intricate practice of the magistrates' procedure was not published until 304 B.C. In 445 intermarriage between the orders was legalised. The richer plebeians also wanted access to the Senate and magistracies. At first, as the plebeians gained ground, the patricians tried to thwart them by creating new magistracies for which plebeians were not eligible; but gradually they were forced to give in. From 367 one consulship was to be held each year by a plebeian. Ten years later the first plebeian was appointed dictator, and before long they could hold the censorship and praetorship. These two offices had been created because of the growing complexity of public business. Censors were responsible for the *census*, the roll of citizens, and they gradually gained a general oversight over public morals, as well as responsibility for revising the list of senators. Praetors were primarily responsible for the administration of justice. Thus in principle the struggle of the orders was over, and the most remarkable aspect of it was that it had been accomplished without bloodshed. Whereas Greek cities had only too often settled their internal differences by civil war (*stasis*), the Romans had shown extraordinary moderation and good sense. Harshness and abuses there must have been, but compromise, even if sometimes long delayed, prevented repetition of the worst excesses of Greek political life. But although victory was won, the result was not quite what might have been expected. Since the plebeians could now hold any office and had entered the Senate in large numbers and since after 287 B.C. they could pass plebiscites that were binding on the whole community, it might have been expected that Rome would soon become a democracy. But in fact the politically successful plebeians made common cause with the patricians. Thus the state continued to be administered by a small body of men, an oligarchy, and this new patricio-plebeian aristocracy proved to be just as exclusive as the older patrician nobility had been. It was drawn from a limited number of families, and men outside this circle had little chance of election to high office or of real influence in state affairs.

While the Romans were busy setting their own house in order, they also had to work out a *modus vivendi* with their neighbours. In early days

Rome had been just one of many Latin settlements and had become a member of a Latin League formed to celebrate certain religious cults in common and for mutual defence. Under the kings in the sixth century Rome had become more powerful than many of its immediate neighbours. This advance was in part due to geographical position. The seven hills over which Rome spread were steeper than they are today and were defensible. The site commanded the ford by the little island in the Tiber, and the river itself was to some extent navigable. Thus Rome was far enough from the sea for protection against raids, while it soon established some control over Ostia at the Tiber's mouth, which later became the port of the city. Thus Rome was well placed to watch any exchange of goods between the hill tribes of the hinterland who would need salt from the coast, while the central position between the two more civilised areas of the Etruscans to the north and the Greeks to the south meant that trade between them by land would be forced to pass through Roman territory. Thus during the Etruscan period Rome had been drawn into a wider world and developed a certain amount of industry and trade; but after the expulsion of the Etruscans it lapsed again into an essentially agricultural community.

During the next two hundred and fifty years Rome extended its influence over the whole of Italy, partly by conquest and partly by building up a confederacy and binding the peoples to itself within the framework of a common political organisation. The details of this great process cannot be given here; but the main lines of advance can be indicated and the resultant confederacy surveyed. As an Etruscan city Rome had become an enemy of the Latins, and after the Etruscan rulers had gone it had to face a war against the Latins. This ended in 493 B.C. at the battle of Lake Regillus, and a treaty was made between Rome on the one side and the Latins on the other, as two independent powers, by which there should be a community of private rights (for example intermarriage and trading facilities) between the citizens of Rome and any Latin city. This sharing of some rights at this early stage was an important contribution by Rome and made possible its further advance. The alliance was not made too soon, because both Rome and the Latins had to face increasing attacks from the hill tribes, the Aequi and Volsci who were pressing down to the more fertile and attractive plain of Latium. Throughout the fifth century the allies kept them at bay and gradually thrust them back. Rome also had to face the hostility of the southernmost Etruscan city,

Veii, which was only fifteen miles away over the Tiber, but after a defeat in 477 B.C. was able to come to terms and thus did not have to fight on the northern frontier as well as to east and south. However, war broke out later, and in 396 Rome finally destroyed Veii.

Six years later the growing state had to face a sterner trial. A marauding band of Celts had come south and defeated the Roman army on the Allia, a tributary of the Tiber some eleven miles from the city, and then swept on and captured Rome itself, except the Capitoline hill. But since these wild Celts had come to plunder rather than to settle, after some months the Romans were able to buy them off. This disaster, however, meant that Roman power was temporarily broken and the Romans had to face further attacks from many of their old enemies – Aequi, Volsci, and Etruscans – and a war against the Latins (340–338) as a result of which the League was broken up and re-organised under Rome's leadership. Next, the Romans clashed in a long series of wars with the Samnites, the main tribe of the central highlands. The chief fighting was between 326 and 290, and was marked by Rome's ignominious setback at the Caudine Forks in 321. However, the Romans finally got the upper hand, and also repelled some further Gallic raids.

These successes were due not merely to military superiority but to wise statecraft. When the Romans defeated an enemy, they might annex part (perhaps a third) of his territory. This they would use in various ways. It might be divided up into small allotments and granted to individual Roman farmers (as was done after the capture of Veii); this helped to drain off the increasing population of Rome and to relieve the economic difficulties of the plebeians. Or the territory might be used to establish a garrison fortress at a strategic point. These colonies were of two kinds. A few were established on the coast and the Roman settlers retained their

Etruscan civilisation, strongly influenced by that of Greece, preceded Roman civilisation in Italy. 120. Etruscan soldier of the 6th cent. B.C. 121. Etruscan jewel-making reached a particularly high standard: fragment of a gold fibula. Much has been learned about the daily life of the Etruscans from numerous finds in tombs hewn out of rocks. 122–3. Burial mounds near the once important Etruscan trading centre of Caere (Cerveteri), situated near the coast to the N. of Rome. 124. Interior of a tomb hewn out of tufa in the cemetery at Cerveteri, with painted stucco utensils, arms, armour, etc., above and between the burial niches. 125. Figure carrying candlestick, an example of Etruscan bronze-casting art. 126. Sarcophagi often bear representations of the dead, in this case a married couple reclining at a meal. 127. Flute-player from the 'Tomb of the Leopards' at Tarquinii.

121

120

122

124

123

125

126

129

130

132

1

3

134

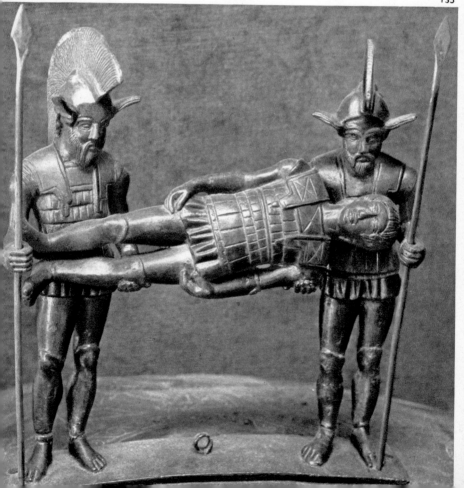

135

Roman citizenship; but more were founded inland and drew their colonists from both Romans and Latins. In these latter colonies (called Latin as opposed to Roman) any Romans renounced their Roman citizenship and became Latins. The Latin colonies were in fact independent states; and it was this network of colonies, bound together by the roads that the Romans constructed throughout Italy, that enabled Rome to control its defeated enemies.

Further, the Romans were very generous in granting their own citizenship to others. Thus, for instance, many whole communities were incorporated in the Roman state when the Latin League was dissolved in 338. And when they thought that a people might be too backward to be granted full Roman citizenship, they might grant it at first some of the privileges of citizenship and then raise it to full citizenship later (for instance the Sabines received 'half citizenship' in 290 and full in 268 B.C.). This graded grant was a wise and helpful method of training more backward tribes to the responsibilities of full citizenship. Where Rome did not grant citizenship, it might make alliances with the conquered. Thus by about 280 B.C. a large part of Italy was either incorporated (in whole or part) in the Roman state or else allied to it, the Latins enjoying especially favoured terms of alliance. Thus Rome had constructed a confederacy bound together by ties of self-interest as well as by feelings of loyalty to Rome. The strength of these bonds was soon to be tested, when a common danger threatened all.

When in 282 B.C. the Greek city of Thurii appealed to Rome for help against the Lucanians, Tarentum objected because it had been accustomed to help the Greek cities of southern Italy against attack from the hill-tribes. The quarrel developed into war, and Tarentum sought help from overseas by appealing to Pyrrhus, the king of Epirus. In 280 he landed in

128. Bronze she-wolf from the Capitol, an Etruscan work, later adopted as a symbol of Rome. There are many mythological accounts of how Rome came to be founded. 130. Third century A.D. relief showing Mars approaching Rhea Silvia who later bore Romulus and Remus, the legendary founders of Rome. 129. An altar depicting the suckling of the twins by the she-wolf. 131. Traces of Rome's early Iron Age inhabitants have been found on the Palatine: floors of huts with holes for piles, dating from the 8th and 7th centuries B.C.; the piles served as supports for roofs. A cinerary urn in the form of a house (132) shows how these earliest houses must have looked. 133. The Capitoline hill at Rome. 134. Agriculture was the basic industry of early Rome: peasant ploughing; an Etruscan bronze. 135. Wars were frequent: the bronze handle of an Etruscan box-lid shows two soldiers carrying a dead comrade.

southern Italy with a large army of professional soldiers, and after a 'Pyrrhic' victory over the Roman forces at Heraclea he marched north in the confident hope that many of Rome's allies would welcome a deliverer. He found, however, that he had misunderstood the nature of the Italian Confederacy: central Italy preferred to remain loyal to Rome and rejected his overtures. After another indecisive battle he went off to help the Sicilian Greeks against the Carthaginians, returning to Italy for a final but unsuccessful trial of strength with Rome in 276. When he withdrew, defeated, Rome made alliances with many of the Greek towns in the south, and strengthened its hold on Italy by establishing more Latin colonies (such as Ariminum and Beneventum in 268 and Aesernia in 263). Thus all Italy south of Cisalpine Gaul was in Rome's hands and had shown that it preferred Rome to Pyrrhus. One reason for this loyalty was that the Romans avoided the mistake that the Athenians had made in their empire: they expected their allies to fight alongside their own legions, but did not demand any payment or taxation from them. Thus the allies could feel that they remained what they were in theory, independent sovereign states. Further, by uniting Italy in this way Rome had created a great power, which to the surprise of the Greek world had defeated one of the outstanding Greek soldiers of the day. The Greeks began to realise that this little-known and backward people of central Italy was becoming a potential world power. But before the Greek world could challenge Rome, trouble arose with the dominant power in the western Mediterranean, Carthage.

ROME AND THE MEDITERRANEAN
(264—133 B.C.)

For a long period the ships of Carthage had dominated the western Mediterranean. Carthage had been founded on a strong natural position on the coast of north Africa by Phoenicians from Tyre about 814 B.C. The Carthaginians belonged to the Semitic race, and spoke a language not unlike the Hebrew of the Old Testament. The city was governed by an oligarchy of nobles, many of whom had made their wealth by trade. It was essentially a commercial city, and while manufacturing some cheap industrial products of its own, carried on a widespread carrier trade and managed to eliminate all commercial rivals from the western Mediterranean, which became its private preserve. To this end it had built up a strong navy, but for land fighting it relied largely on mercenary troops. Its contribution to civilisation was not great, since its art was uninspiring, its religion cruel, and its literature probably negligible. The Carthaginians had gradually extended their influence along the coast of north Africa to the straits of Gibraltar (the Pillars of Hercules), and then to southern Spain, Sardinia, and western Sicily. In general they seem to have achieved this empire without great difficulty, but in Sicily they were in constant conflict with the Greek cities who had settled the eastern part of the island (see pp. 68, 98); one recent phase in the struggle had been marked by the intervention of Pyrrhus (p. 129).

Since the early Romans were far-mers with little interest in overseas trade, there was no reason why their relations with Carthage should not be friendly, and in fact they had been quite willing to make a treaty in 509 B.C. by which they promised not to interfere in Carthaginian waters. But when Rome had united the whole of Italy, and had as allies some of the Greek cities of the south, who had commercial interests, the situation began to change. Trouble developed when both peoples became interested in the control of Messana, which dominated the straits between Italy and Sicily. Probably neither side

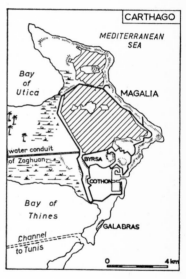

planned war, but each was eager to deny to the other control of the straits, and in 264 B.C. they found themselves at war.

The Romans sent an army to Sicily, where with the help of Hieron II, the king of Syracuse, they occupied the eastern part of the island and cap-tured Agrigentum. Then a problem arose: if the Romans decided to drive the Carthaginians completely out of Sicily, they would have to smash the Punic navy, and that was no easy task because they had virtually no ships of their own. However, they were a practical as well as a deter-mined people, and so they set to work and built a fleet of over 100 ships. Even more surprising was the fact that when this fleet went into action for the first time, off Mylae, it defeated the Carthaginian fleet; this was due partly to the adoption of a kind of boarding-bridge (*corvus*, 'crow') which enabled the Romans to make sea battles more like land battles.

After this victory in 260, the Romans sent a force to attack Carthage itself. This daring adventure ended in disaster when the expeditionary force under Regulus was defeated in Africa. Thereafter the war dragged on, as neither side would give in. There was much fighting in Sicily, where at last the Romans managed to confine their enemies to the western fortresses of Drepana and Lilybaeum, while renewed Roman efforts by sea met with many a disaster, but more as a result of storm and shipwreck than of enemy action. At last in 241 B.C. the Romans won a decisive naval battle at the Aegates Islands just off the west end of Sicily, and the Punic commander Hamilcar Barca had to capitulate. By the terms of the treaty the Carthaginians agreed to evacuate Sicily as well as to pay Rome an indemnity, but they remained an independent power.

The Romans thus found that they had Sicily on their hands, although they almost certainly had not started the war to achieve such a result. While leaving Hieron in control of his kingdom of Syracuse, they made the rest of the island into a *provincia*, which strictly meant merely the sphere in which a Roman magistrate exercised his *imperium*. Before long the Romans sent out a praetor each year to administer the island, which had to pay an annual tax to Rome in the form of a tithe on harvested crops. The Romans did not create a new civil service to collect the taxes, but left the task to individuals who were granted the right to act.

Further trouble developed between Rome and Carthage when in 238 the Romans seized Sardinia and thus embittered relations once again. The island was organised as Rome's second overseas province in 227. But the Romans had other trouble nearer home. In 236 their northern frontier had been threatened by Gallic tribes, and ten years later a crisis arose when the Boii swept down into Italy. Men remembered how Gallic tribes had sacked Rome in 390 B.C. But the Romans managed skilfully to manoeuvre the Gallic army between two of their own armies at Telamon and there defeated them. The Romans also had to keep a lookout across the Adriatic, where Illyrian pirates preyed on passing shipping. Two short campaigns (230–228, 221–219) sufficed to defeat the Illyrians, but Rome made no attempt to extend its empire into the Balkans.

More serious trouble flared up in Spain. Hamilcar Barca after the First Punic War had extended Carthaginian conquests in Spain; but although

the Romans objected, diplomatic moves averted war until in 219 Hamilcar's son Hannibal, who had succeeded to the command, besieged Saguntum, a city that had an alliance with Rome. The Romans, preoccupied
with Illyria, allowed their ally to fall to Hannibal and then in 218 sent an
ultimatum to Carthage which resulted in a declaration of war. This
they hoped to be able to fight in their own way, and they planned to

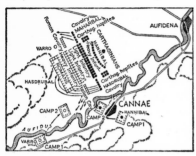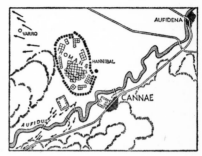

Battle of Cannae (216 B.C.). *Left*, the battle order; *right*, Hannibal's encircling movement
completed.

send one army to deal with Hannibal in Spain and a second to attack
Carthage in Africa. But their plans were upset by the bold strategy of
Hannibal, who determined to strike at Italy itself and thus paralyse
the Roman efforts. He marched from Spain to Gaul, where he turned
up the Rhône valley just before a Roman army could stop him, and then
made his famous crossing of the Alps and arrived with some 26,000 men in
northern Italy. Victory followed victory: at the Trebia, at Lake Trasimene, where he trapped a large Roman army, and finally in 216 at Cannae,
where his superior cavalry and greater tactical flexibility enabled him
to inflict on the Romans the greatest defeat in their history.

Yet they refused to admit themselves beaten; and this was partly because Hannibal's plans had not in fact worked out quite as he had hoped.
Like Pyrrhus before him, he had believed that if once he could get to
Italy Rome's allies there would be only too willing to desert it and
join his cause. In this he completely miscalculated, and so far the Confederacy had supported Rome. After Cannae, however, parts of southern
Italy, including the great city of Capua (and ultimately Tarentum and
Syracuse) did go over to him; but central Italy remained loyal to Rome,
who doggedly fought on. Thanks to Rome's superior naval power,
reinforcements failed to reach Hannibal, and gradually his strength was
worn down. His last hope was when in 207 his brother Hasdrubal managed

to bring an army from Spain to join him, but the Romans anticipated events and succeeded in defeating Hasdrubal at the river Metaurus in northern Italy before he could reach Hannibal in the south.

Meantime the Romans had grimly tried to prevent reinforcements coming from Spain, where they had attempted to confine the Punic forces. After some setbacks young Publius Cornelius Scipio was sent out to command the Roman forces there, and he gradually turned the tide of battle. He captured the Punic base at New Carthage (Cartagena) in 209 and finally by a victory at Ilipa near Seville swept the enemy right out of Spain (206). Meantime the Carthaginians had persuaded Philip V king of Macedon to support them, and Rome was thus forced to send troops to fight in the Balkans, but this First Macedonian War ended successfully in 205. Now the Romans were able to make their final effort. They sent an army to Africa (204) under the command of Scipio who won a series of victories and thus compelled Carthage to recall Hannibal from Italy. At the final battle called 'Zama' (it was fought some 75 miles inland southwest of Carthage), thanks to tactical reforms which he had introduced into his army, Scipio was able to achieve final victory and bring the long war to an end. By the terms of the peace (202) Carthage had to give up everything outside an area roughly equivalent to that of modern Tunisia, to surrender its fleet, and to pay an indemnity. But once again it was left as an independent sovereign state. Scipio on his return home received the name Africanus.

Scarcely was this life-and-death struggle over when Rome became involved in war with the Hellenistic world, where the balance of power had been upset by the aggressions of Philip of Macedon and Antiochus the Great of Syria. As a result of Philip's threats to Greek cities in Asia and Greece, Roman help was sought, and the war-weary Romans sent a force once again to Greece in 200 B.C., where they finally defeated Philip at Cynoscephalae in Thessaly. They did not, however, wish to get permanently involved in Greece, and so the Roman armies went home; but before long they were recalled through the aggression of Antiochus. For some time this ruler had been trying to win back a portion of the Eastern conquests of his Seleucid predecessors on the Syrian throne, and in 191 he invaded Greece. The Romans defeated him at Thermopylae and crossed over to Asia to inflict a final defeat on him at Magnesia. They allowed both these kings, Philip and Antiochus, to retain their thrones, but they circumscribed their territories. In particular the island of Rhodes and the kingdom of Pergamum benefited from Syria's defeat, because Rome still determined not to undertake direct responsibility for Greek affairs. When Philip's son and successor, Perseus, gave trouble the Romans intervened, defeated him at Pydna (168), and deposed him; but they turned Macedon into four republics. Only in 146, after a pretender to the Macedonian throne named Andriscus had led a national uprising, did the Romans finally decide to administer Greece themselves by establishing Macedon as a province. The Greeks had for sixty years been quarrelling among themselves, and now at last they had peace imposed upon them, but at the price of their independence, as Corinth in particular realised when the city was sacked by Rome.

About this same time Rome became involved with Carthage once more. On this occasion the Romans acted with great brutality, and after a brief war in which Carthage gallantly resisted siege by a Roman army and navy the survivors were forced to capitulate. The city was destroyed, in accordance with the policy that Cato had advocated, and the Romans determined to have no more Punic wars. They annexed the territory of Carthage (roughly Tunisia) as a new province named Africa (146). But they had also to watch their northern and western frontiers. The Gauls, who had given Hannibal some help, were punished, and their land was settled with colonies (among others Bononia in 189, Mutina and Parma in 183). Then the flanks of Cisalpine Gaul were guarded by the defeat of the Istri and the founding of Aquileia (near Trieste) and the reduction of the Dalmatians and the Ligurians. Finally, there was Spain. After driving out the Carthaginians, the Romans had organised Spain as two provinces in 197, but they had not conquered the centre and north. In a long series of wars the Celtiberians of the upper Ebro valley and the Lusitanians in the west were gradually reduced, despite the heroic resistance of the Lusitanian leader Viriathus and the stubborn resistance of the Celtiberian capital of Numantia to a Roman siege which ended in its final destruction in 133.

In this way Roman power was established without threat of serious challenge throughout the Mediterranean and the Romans had acquired five provinces as a result of their struggles with Carthage (Sicily, Sardinia together with Corsica, Nearer and Further Spain, and Africa), to which they added another in Macedonia. In 133 Attalus the king of Pergamum died and bequeathed his kingdom to Rome; this was accepted and became the province of Asia. Thus Rome's Mediterranean empire was created and guarded. It was administered by annual governors sent out from Rome to each province. The governor was responsible for the general administration of law and order, and since he was away from possible supervision by a colleague in Rome he might acquire considerable power, especially if he had any troops in his province. But in these early days on the whole governors seem to have been restrained, administration was fairly upright, and the collection of the taxes (which except in Sicily and Asia were fixed sums), though left to private tax-gatherers (*publicani*), did not lead at first to grave abuses.

EARLY ROMAN LIFE AND CULTURE

Rome had gone through many phases: a shepherds' village, an Etruscan city, a member of a Latin League, the leader of an Italian Confederacy, the mistress of a Mediterranean empire, a world power. Social, cultural, and economic life obviously changed greatly during these years, but such changes were fairly gradual until the pace was accelerated through the consequences of the Hannibalic War. Agriculture was the chief industry of the Roman people; the peasant-farmer was the mainstay of the state, and the government was in the hands of a landed aristocracy. With Rome's conquest of Italy the earlier more progressive economic life in Etruria and Magna Graecia tended to become more simplified, and Italy became in the main a nation of small farmers. But the conquest of the Mediterranean had serious repercussions. Many men, enriched by war or trade, began to buy up land as an investment. This led to an increase in large estates (*latifundia*), which were often devoted more to pasturage than corn growing and were worked increasingly

136–7. Two archaic terracotta heads: a maenad from a temple on the Capitoline hill, and a bearded deity from Satricum. / 138. Alba Fucens, founded in 303 B.C., typifies the spread of Roman power: view of the citadel on a hill within the walls. 139. The 'cyclopean' walls are characteristic of many cities built about this period. 140. Course, within the city, of the Via Valeria, the main road from Rome to the east coast. 141–2. Hannibal's African elephants on Carthaginian coins minted in Spain. The clash with Carthage was a turning-point in Rome's history. 143. Saguntum: its siege and capture by Hannibal led to the Second Punic War. 144. An important ally of Rome in this struggle was Hieron, king of Syracuse. 148. The defeat at Cannae by the Carthaginians created a serious crisis for Rome: view of the site of Cannae.

136

137

138

139

140

141 142

143

144

145

146

147

150

149

151

152

153

154

155

156

157

with the slave labour that the wars had made more readily available.

This supersession of peasant husbandry by capitalist farming in many parts of Italy in the second century resulted in much hardship for the smaller farmers, who were often forced from their farms by economic pressure and migrated to the big towns, especially Rome, where they failed to find employment. There was no expanding industry to absorb them. Industry in Italy after the Etruscan period and the flourishing days of the Greek cities had tended to be local and limited. Naturally all the everyday objects that were needed in the home, in agriculture, and in the army, were manufactured, and these would be sold in local markets or shops; the shopkeeper, however, generally made and sold his goods in the same room. Little attempt was made to build up large industries for export purposes. This was partly because Romans of good family left industry to the lower classes, who would lack capital. Further, Rome had little interest in overseas trade before gaining an overseas empire. Again, social factors were involved. Senators belonged to a landed nobility that did not favour trade, and by a law of 218 B.C. they were actually forbidden to become traders. This had far-reaching consequences. Trade became the monopoly of a separate class in the state, the *Equites* or equestrian order. Some of these men might come from the same families as senators, but by choosing a life of commerce they automatically cut themselves off from a public career. Thus a sharp distinction developed between the senatorial order and those who enriched themselves by industry, commerce, or banking.

Family life, as already said, was a very strong bond among the early Romans, and education was very much a family concern. Character was formed by the example of the parents, home life, and ancestral custom (*mos maiorum*). But changes came. Divorce began to be known. About

In the East the Romans expanded their Empire after defeating the Macedonians at Pydna in 168 B.C. This victory was commemorated by the erection at Delphi of a monument showing Macedonians (round shields) and Romans in combat (146). About a century earlier, attempts to conquer Italy from the east by Pyrrhus, in which Indian elephants (147) were used, had been foiled. In the following century the fight against the peoples in the West was decided under the leadership of Julius Caesar. The triumphal arch at Orange (149) commemorated victory over the Gauls. 148. The side of this arch, with representations of captured weapons, Gallic prisoners, etc. 180. Gallic warrior, an enemy of Rome at this period. 151. Sulla. 152. Marcus Antonius. 153. Lepidus. 154. Brutus. 155. Reverse of 154: cap of liberty with two daggers and the 'Ides of March'. 156. Pompeius Magnus. 187. Gaius Julius Caesar.

250 B.C. the first school was opened in Rome. Slavery gradually increased. In early days slaves were not numerous, and they could often obtain their freedom; a slave's status might not be much inferior to that of a servant, and he would work alongside his master in the fields. But conquest led to a great increase in the numbers of slaves and to deterioration in the treatment of them.

One of the most potent factors that promoted change in Roman life was Hellenism. During the regal period the Romans had seen something of Greek art through contact with Etruria and Campania, but thereafter they had lapsed into a parochial state until their soldiers visited Greek cities in Sicily during the First Punic War and Greece itself during the Second. Such contacts awakened in many Romans the consciousness that they had no literature, philosophy, or great art of their own, and they began to admire and imitate Greek models. Many Roman nobles, such as the Scipios and Flamininus, became ardent philhellenists, and Greek ideas and manners began to affect all aspects of Roman life in the second century. Some old-fashioned Romans felt that these new ideas might undermine older Roman standards of conduct and morality. But although Cato might check the tide he could not stop it; and later (soon after 150 B.C.) a group of thinkers and writers gathered round Scipio Aemilianus. One such was Polybius, a Greek exile from Megalopolis, who wrote a universal history describing Rome's expansion throughout the Mediterranean world and showing how this had for the first time in history introduced a unity into world history. The members of this so-called Scipionic Circle tried to blend the better elements in the Greek and Roman traditions. How these Greek ideas affected various aspects of life and thought must now be briefly considered.

Literature was a late development in Roman life. If there was early ballad poetry, it did not survive; the beginnings of Latin prose can be seen in official documents such as the Twelve Tables, and the habit of speech in the Senate and the delivery of formal funeral orations stimulated the growth of oratory. But Rome had virtually no literature before the mid-third century. Poetry started from translation from Greek: Livius Andronicus (ca. 284–204) translated the *Odyssey* into Latin in a metre called Saturnian; he also translated some Greek tragedies and comedies. Naevius then composed an account of the First Punic War in Saturnians. But the greatest of the early poets was Ennius (239–169), who not only adapted Greek tragedies and comedies but wrote an epic account of Rome from early times down to 172 B.C. in hexameter verse. Plautus (254–184) and Terence (195–159) specialised in comedy and skilfully adapted plays of the New Comedy of Athens for production on the Roman stage. The humour of Plautus was much more robust and knockabout than the refined and elegant approach of Terence. When the Romans began to want to record their own history, they actually wrote in Greek. Thus some senators such as Fabius Pictor about 200 B.C. began to write histories of Rome. They were soon followed by Cato, who wrote in Latin and

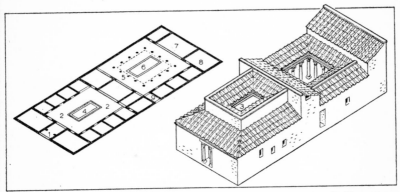

Reconstruction of a Roman house. 1. Vestibulum (entrance); 2. Atrium (hall); 3. Compluvium (rain cistern); 4. Impluvium (shallow basin); 5. Peristylium (innercourt); 6. Piscina (fish-pond); 7. Exedra (garden room); 8. Triclinium (dining-room); 9. Posticum (back door); Remainder: living-rooms, bedrooms, and servants' quarters.

may be regarded as the father of Latin prose; besides history, he wrote on many subjects and published a large number of his speeches. Thus a wide range of literature was produced; some of the writers touched heights of greatness, and although they owed an immeasurable debt to Greece their work soon showed a true reflection of their own national character.

It was much the same story in the sphere of art. In the regal period Rome had seen something of Etruscan and Greek art, and temples in these traditions had been built in the city and adorned with cult-statues and other decorations. But thereafter Rome entered into a more austere period when men had little time for artistic pursuits. However, the native Italic traditions survived, not least in skill in portraiture, and were reawakened by contact with the Greek world. Not only were Greek works of art displayed in Rome, such as those captured from Syracuse in 211 B.C., but knowledge of Greek cities stimulated fresh architectural desires, and in the second century Rome began to assume a new appearance.

147

New temples were built in the Hellenistic manner with walls of tufa covered with bright stucco, basilicas and porticoes arose, and private houses became less austere.

In early days the Romans believed in impersonal spirits (*numina*) which lived in springs, trees, or stones and others which watched over all the varied activities of human life from birth to death. Religious practice centred around the family, the house, and the farm, and such spirits as that of the fire on the hearth (Vesta) received simple worship. But under Etruscan and Greek influences the Romans began to think of the gods in human form, to build temples for them, and to make statues of them; in other words, simple animistic beliefs were replaced by anthropomorphic conceptions. At the same time the state stepped in and undertook certain public cults and ceremonies designed to preserve the goodwill of heaven, the *pax deorum*. Provided these public sacrifices and prayers were duly carried out, the ordinary man needed to worry little about religion, and a formalised state cult tended to overshadow the growth of more genuine personal religious feelings. These found outlet in the cults of the home and countryside, and later in the reception of foreign cults, not only those of Greece but (after ca. 200 B.C.) some from Asia Minor, such as that of the Great Mother Goddess of Phrygia. But although some of these cults appealed to the needs of the individual, many stirred up emotional frenzy which was repugnant to the serious commonsense outlook of the older Roman. Some attempts were made to check these foreign cults, yet they gradually made headway in Italy. Many Romans reacted in a similar way to their first contacts with Greek philosophy, and even expelled from Rome two Epicurean philosophers in 173 B.C. But many of the Roman nobles turned eagerly to this new source of enlightenment, and both Stoicism and Epicureanism gained an increasing influence over Roman thought after about 150 B.C.

In one great sphere of thought and practice, however, the Romans owed very little to the Greeks, but in turn put the later world deeply in their debt. One of the great achievements of the Roman mind was its conception and development of law. Without the authority of a divine lawgiver, as with the Jews, or of a human lawgiver, as with many Greek states, a small community of farmers succeeded from an inherent sense of justice and equity in establishing a body of law which found its first publication in the Twelve Tables in the mid-fifth century. This was a remarkable achievement. These statutes were gradually modified to meet fresh needs by constant reinterpretation (cf. precedent in English Common Law, that is, principles established by individual judges); this was done at first by the college of pontiffs, and then by a class of jurists who gave their advice free. They were not professional lawyers, but Roman nobles who regarded jurisprudence as part of the art of government. It may be noted that the Romans avoided professionalism in their priesthoods also: the two main priestly colleges, of pontiffs and augurs, were not a priestly caste, but were composed of ordinary Roman nobles. But while the Romans built up their Civil Law for their own citizens, they had also to deal with other peoples, at first in Italy and then abroad. Largely as the result of the action of Roman magistrates, praetors in Rome and provincial governors abroad, a system was devised which applied to all free men, irrespective of nationality. Thus the *ius gentium* was evolved, 'that part of the law which we apply to ourselves and to foreigners', and the legal system was gradually extended to meet ever-widening needs.

THE FALL OF THE REPUBLIC

The Senate was the effective, though not the constitutional, government of Rome, and its control had hitherto not been seriously challenged. Its resolution during the Hannibalic War had added to its authority, and in general the people acquiesced in its direction, including even the tribunes, who had tended to become like the regular magistrates and to carry out the Senate's wishes. But during the second century many tensions developed in the state, not least through the changing economic situation (see p. 136), which led to unemployment. Reform was attempted by Tiberius Gracchus, who was tribune in 133 B.C. He proposed an agrarian law to compel large landowners to surrender any *ager publicus* (land belonging to the state) which they were holding in excess of a legal limit that had in fact been disregarded for some time; this land was to be distributed in small allotments to unemployed Roman citizens who had lost their farms. Gracchus perhaps overestimated the probable resistance of the Senate and decided to bypass the normal procedure of bringing his bill before it. He took it direct to the people, who went so far as to depose another of the tribunes who tried to veto it. At this point Attalus of Pergamum bequeathed his kingdom to Rome (p. 135), and Gracchus proposed to devote some of this legacy to help his new settlers. Now, all this involved a direct challenge to the Senate, which normally handled finance and foreign affairs, and the opposition to Gracchus hardened. When he stood for re-election for a second tribunate, rioting broke out and the Senate's action led to the deaths of Gracchus and many of his followers. This marked a turning point in Rome's history. Hitherto internal differences had been settled by peaceful means, but now the Senate had used force to suppress a genuine reformer, whose methods had been extremely provocative but perhaps not technically illegal.

Ten years later Tiberius' brother, Gaius Gracchus, came forward to continue his brother's work. He held the tribunate for two years (123–122) and carried a large number of reforms. He ensured that the agrarian bill should continue to function, he won popular support by arranging that the state should sell corn at under the market price and by establishing new colonies in Italy (and one abroad, at Carthage), and he secured the backing of the business classes (the equestrian order) by arranging that they should collect the taxes of the new province of Asia and also have control of the permanent court that had recently been established in Rome to try provincial governors who were charged with maladministration. In all this he was not seeking personal power but rather the political backing that would enable him to tackle one of the most urgent problems of the day, which, if not resolved, might lead to civil war in Italy. This was the relation of Rome and its allies, whose loyalty, which had withstood the assaults of Hannibal, now began to weaken since Rome's treatment of them had deteriorated. Gracchus proposed that the Latins should be given Roman citizenship and the rest of the allies should get Latin rights. This suggestion provoked great resentment at Rome, and once again the Senate used force to suppress the reformer: Gaius and some 3,000 followers were killed or put to death after a nominal trial. Thus the power of the Senate had withstood these assaults, but the Gracchi had achieved much: many small farmers had been set up again, the people had learned how to challenge the Senate, the equestrian order had gained considerable political influence at the expense of the Senate, and the Italian allies were disappointed and eager to press their claims.

The next attack on the Senate's authority came from Marius as the result of difficulties overseas. There had been some trouble in southern Gaul, where the Romans had intervened to protect Massilia from attacks by Gallic tribes. As a result the district around Narbo, where the Romans had established a colony in 118, was annexed as a new Roman province called Gallia Narbonensis. There had earlier been a revolt of slaves in Sicily (135-132); but in general the provinces were peaceful until Jugurtha, a Numidian prince, claimed the throne of Numidia (roughly Algeria). The Romans sent an army to Africa against him in 112; but the war dragged on until Gaius Marius, who was serving there, went home and persuaded the people to elect him consul for 107 and to give him the command in Africa, thereby disregarding the wishes of the Senate. Further, Marius took with him to Africa an army of volunteers, however poor. This was a great innovation. Hitherto the Roman army had been raised only from those citizens that had some property to defend (men enrolled in the five *classes*); after a campaign they would be eager to get back to their farms. Now Marius had an army of landless men who after the war would look to him to make some provision for them, preferably in the form of land. Till now the army had been raised by and owed loyalty to the state alone; but now a dangerous nexus of personal interest bound an army to its own commander. This might, and did in fact, lead to the rise of military dictators who threatened and finally helped to overthrow the Republic.

Marius soon managed to defeat Jugurtha and bring the war to an end. In this he was helped by the diplomatic skill of one of his officers, Lucius Cornelius Sulla, who negotiated Jugurtha's surrender. No major changes were made in Africa. Soon, however, Rome had to face a more serious menace. Germanic tribes were on the move in central Europe and defeated Roman armies in Austria in 113 and at Arausio (Orange) in the Rhône valley in 105; they then threatened Italy itself. To meet this emergency Marius was elected to a second consulship for 104 to face them, but when they held back he was re-elected each year. This interval enabled him to introduce some important reforms in the Roman army before he finally met and defeated the Teutones at Aquae Sextiae (Aix) in southern Gaul in 102 and the Cimbri at Vercellae in northern Italy in 101. He then returned to Rome in triumph to hold his sixth consulship in 100. However, he proved less successful in politics than in war. He got into the hands of two demagogues, but when he found that they were ready to try to challenge the Senate by force he withdrew his support and they were soon crushed. This left him in a weak position, since he had failed as a popular leader and the Senate no longer needed to worry about him.

But grave trouble arose some ten years later. A tribune, Drusus, in 91 raised the franchise question once more, and when he was murdered the

Italian allies decided to break away from Rome, set up an independent state, and fight for their liberty. A grim Social War raged for two years or more, in which the Romans managed to survive but won victory only by granting to the Italians what they wanted, namely Roman citizenship. This settlement marks a decisive stage in Roman history: henceforth all the peoples of Italy (south of Cisalpine Gaul) were full Roman citizens, and Italy was at last politically united as one nation.

The course of foreign affairs, however, prevented Rome from settling down. Mithridates, the king of Pontus in Asia Minor, in 88 overran the Roman province of Asia, massacring 80,000 Romans and Italians and calling on the Greek cities to revolt from Rome. He then sent an army and fleet to Greece. To meet this threat the Senate had appointed Sulla as commander in the East, but a tribune, Sulpicius Rufus, proposed that the command should be transferred to Marius. Sulla refused to recognise this and marched on Rome with six legions. His enemies fled, and he passed some measures to strengthen the Senate, and then went off to defeat Mithridates' armies in Greece. While he was away the popular party got the upper hand and massacred many of its opponents, but Marius died when consul for the seventh time in 86, and the popular leaders settled down to await Sulla's return. Before long he had brought Mithridates to terms, and after landing in southern Italy in 83 he fought his way to supremacy in a civil war that lasted until 82. In this he was helped by Pompey and Crassus, two men of the future. After getting rid of political opponents in another proscription he arranged that he should be named dictator. He carried through a number of reforms designed to strengthen the authority of the Senate: thus he checked the powers of the censors and other magistrates and of the tribunes, arranged that the provinces should be governed by promagistrates (that is, men

The development of Roman art. **158.** The importance attached to family ties finds its expression in many (mainly Republican) funerary steles with representations of families. **159.** Bust of a Roman, an example of the high standard of Republican portraiture. **160.** Roman temple at Nîmes, built shortly before our era on a podium, as was the Roman usage. **161.** The Forum Boarium at Rome shows an almost intact part of Republican Rome: a circular temple, remains of a house (in background), and the temple of Fortuna Virilis. **162–3.** Frescoes, stucco work, etc., still give some impression of the lavish construction and appointments of Roman houses, which were often provided with architectural wall decorations, not only for embellishment but also to create an illusion of size. **164.** The Gemma Augustea, showing Augustus and the goddess Roma with Tiberius and personified figures.

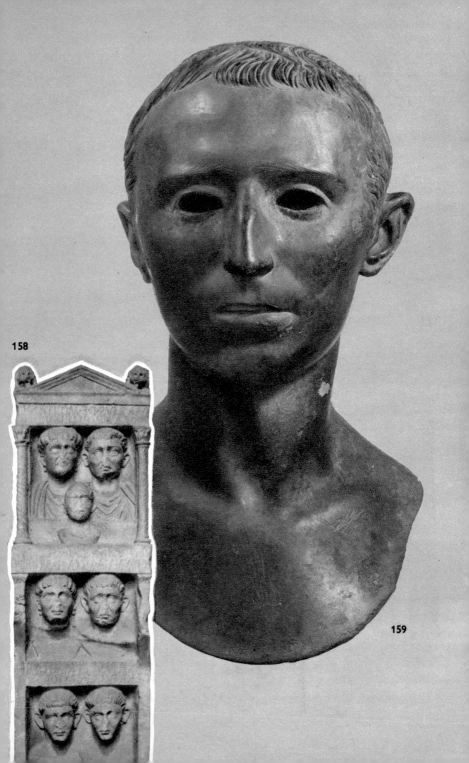

158

159

2

3

164

165

166

169

170

who had held office in Rome the previous year), passed a law about treason which limited the powers of provincial governors, and introduced some judicial reforms establishing seven permanent criminal courts which were to be empanelled by senators. He thus tried to safeguard the Senate from attacks by ambitious tribunes with the people behind them or ambitious promagistrates with armies behind them. He resigned his dictatorship in 79 and died the next year.

The Senate, thus reinforced, met with increasing difficulties in trying to conduct domestic and foreign affairs. At home a counter-revolution, led by Lepidus, the consul of 78, was crushed, but there was mounting pressure for the restoration of full powers to the tribunes. In the East the balance of power was upset when Rome accepted Bithynia as a legacy from its king (75 B.C.); this led Mithridates to take to the war-path again, and he was only gradually beaten back. Piracy, which had increased in the eastern Mediterranean, especially around Crete and the coast of Cilicia, gave much trouble. In Spain Sertorius, one of Marius' supporters who had left Italy to fight on elsewhere, kept the senatorial generals at bay; even when Pompey was sent against him in 77 the war was not won until after his murder in 73. Finally, Spartacus raised a slave revolt and overran southern Italy and defeated the armies sent against him until Crassus finally overcame him in 71. Thus in all these spheres the senatorial administration showed its weakness; and when Pompey and Crassus at the head of their armies returned to Rome and demanded the consulship for 70 B.C., the Senate had to yield. Former lieutenants of Sulla, they now proceeded to sweep away most of his reforms, and thus left a weakened Senate exposed to further attack. Neither, however, sought illegally to prolong his period of power or even to go to a province. But they did not remain inactive for long.

Many events in, and aspects of, Roman history are recorded in reliefs. **165.** Detail of the frieze from the Ara Pacis, showing priests and members of Augustus' family. **166.** The senate, symbolised by a bearded man, and the Roman people, in the form of a young man with a cornucopia. The architecture of the Romans attained great perfection in amphitheatres, aqueducts, arches, etc. **167.** The famous Pont du Gard aqueduct in southern France. **168.** Many triumphal arches were built, either simple like that at Susa to Augustus (shown here) or more ambitious as in later Imperial times (see **172–3**). The art of mosaic contributed much to the decoration and magnificence of public and private buildings, and also reveals many aspects of Roman life. **169.** Still life. **170.** A rustic scene. **171.** Fragment of a late 3rd cent. A.D. sarcophagus with excellent rendering of features and drapery.

A fresh crisis soon summoned Pompey from retirement. In 67 the pirate menace had become so threatening that the people decided to entrust Pompey with extraordinary powers to deal with it. This was proposed by a tribune Gabinius against the wishes of the Senate, and was precisely the kind of measure that Sulla had tried to make impossible by his muzzling of the tribunate. Pompey did a fine job, and cleared the seas in three months instead of the three years that he had been allotted. But Mithridates was not yet subdued. Lucullus had driven him from Pontus and then defeated his son-in-law Tigranes the king of Armenia (74–68). But Lucullus' just financial administration annoyed the Equites, who worked for his supersession. In 66 another tribune, Manilius, proposed that Pompey should be given full powers to settle the East. This Pompey did efficiently. He finally defeated Mithridates, annexed Syria as a new province, and reorganised the various native kingdoms of central Asia Minor as 'client kingdoms' of Rome, founding a number of new cities there. These kingdoms would act as buffer-states between the Roman provinces and the menacing kingdom of Parthia beyond the Euphrates.

Meantime in Pompey's absence men in Rome began to wonder how he would use his immense powers when he came back. Crassus and young Julius Caesar began to intrigue against his return, knowing that he would need land on which to settle his veteran troops; but they failed to achieve their designs. The situation was complicated by the attempt of Catiline, a bankrupt noble, to overthrow the state and the existing order; this conspiracy was unmasked and prevented by Cicero, who won the consulship for 63 although he did not come from an old senatorial family. Pompey when he returned in triumph to Italy at the end of 62 made no attempt to seize power, and Cicero began to hope that the more moderate elements that had rallied against Catiline might be bound together in a *concordia ordinum* with Pompey's approval. But he failed to achieve this, partly because of the opposition of the diehard senators, the Optimates, who by thwarting both Pompey and Crassus and Caesar drove these three to work together in a political alliance known as the First Triumvirate.

These men, with Pompey's veterans in the background, forced through their wishes, including a consulship for Caesar in 59, which was to be followed for him by a command in Gaul. Here there was considerable unrest, since the Helvetii were on the move seeking new homes, and the

German chief Ariovistus had settled down west of the Rhine. Caesar proceeded to conquer the whole of Gaul in a series of brilliant campaigns and added it as a new province, Transalpine Gaul. But meanwhile his relations with Pompey and Crassus deteriorated, despite an attempt to patch them up at a conference at Luca (56). Crassus, after he had held the consulship again with Pompey in 55, went off to attack the Parthians in the East. This attempt ended in disaster: his army was smashed at Carrhae in 53 and he was killed. Thus a link between Pompey and Caesar was broken, and they drifted further apart. The details of this quarrel cannot be described here, but it was embittered by the declining standard of political life at Rome, which was dominated by the struggles of two gang leaders, Clodius and Milo, who were reducing politics to ochlocracy. Finally, Caesar, who had been manoeuvred into an impossible political position, crossed the Rubicon, the northern frontier of Italy, with his army, and civil war had begun (49).

The speed with which Caesar advanced forced Pompey to evacuate Italy and to try to build up his forces in Greece. But as Pompey also had forces in Spain (since 55 he had been governor but had administered his province by deputy), Caesar struck at these first, defeating the main army at Ilerda (49) and securing the whole peninsula. He then went on to Greece. After some critical manoeuvring against Pompey at Dyrrhachium on the west coast, he withdrew to Thessaly where he finally defeated Pompey at Pharsalus (48). Pompey fled to Egypt, where he was murdered; Caesar followed and spent the winter in Alexandria with Cleopatra, who after the death of her brother became queen of Egypt. Two further campaigns remained against the surviving supporters of Pompey. Those who had mustered in Africa were defeated by Caesar at the battle of Thapsus (46), while the remnants who fled to Spain, where two of Pompey's sons were organising resistance, were defeated at Munda (45). Caesar, who had paid several hasty visits to Rome during these years, was now free to return for good. He held various offices. He had been elected consul each year from 48 to 44 except 47, but the main basis of his authority was the dictatorship, which he had received in varying forms but which in 44 he was granted for life. During his short periods in Rome he had introduced a great number of reforms: the calendar was adjusted (the Julian calender remained in use in Britain until the eighteenth century); he planned many public works and buildings in Rome and Italy; he established many colonies for his veterans and the poor outside Italy (for example at Carthage and Corinth), he granted Roman citizenship widely; and he planned to protect the frontiers of the empire by campaigns against the Dacians (who lived north of the Danube, in modern Romania) and against the Parthians. But before he could set off on these he was murdered. In the last months of his life his conduct became somewhat autocratic, while the honours that he received offended the older nobility, of which after all Caesar himself was only a fellow-member. Thus a conspiracy was formed to remove the man whom some regarded as a tyrant and to restore the Republic. On the Ides of March 44 Caesar was assassinated.

Many of the conspirators had acted from high motives, but they were very short-sighted. They seem to have imagined that if Caesar was removed the old Republic would function once again. But in fact there was little hope of this: mortal blows had already been struck at it by the selfish Optimate clique, by scheming politicians who had used force, and by generals who commanded armies that were more ready to serve them than the state. Thus Caesar's death merely plunged the Roman world into thirteen more years of civil war.

Antony, Caesar's lieutenant, soon drove Brutus and Cassius and other conspirators from Rome, but his claims were challenged by young Octavian who had been adopted as Caesar's heir. While Octavian raised forces, Cicero denounced Antony in a series of speeches (the *Philippics*), and Antony was declared a public enemy and defeated in battle. But the Senate's treatment of Octavian led him to compromise with Antony, and together with Lepidus they were duly elected as triumvirs (the Second Triumvirate) in 43. They then got rid of their political opponents in Rome by a ghastly proscription and crossed to Greece and defeated the forces of Brutus and Cassius at Philippi (42). Antony and Octavian, ignoring Lepidus, in effect divided the Roman world between them. The West fell to Octavian, who in the next six years eliminated all rivals, including Lepidus and Sextus Pompeius, a son of Pompey. Meantime Antony had gone to the East, where he met Cleopatra and ultimately launched a disastrous campaign against the Parthians. He then went to join Cleopatra at Alexandria and became increasingly identified with traditions of the East, while Octavian gained strength from his championship of the traditions of Rome, Italy, and the West. With the world divided between them, the final clash could scarcely be averted. It came at the battle of Actium in 31; Antony fled with Cleopatra to Egypt, where they soon committed suicide. Thus Octavian had conquered all rivals and was master of the whole Roman world. The problem that faced him was whether he could retain power and how to use it: could the Republic be restored or orderly government be re-established?

LIFE IN THE DAYS OF CICERO

During the late Republic standards of public and social life changed considerably. The governing class became wealthier, and although many men maintained the honourable ways of earlier days, many became corrupted in the race for wealth and position. Luxury, display, and extravagance increased. Besides their fashionable town houses, many nobles now had numerous villas on country estates, especially by the sea. But the heart of Roman society was in Rome itself, with social pleasures and duties from the early morning *salutatio* when clients waited on their noble patron to pay their respects or seek his help, to fashionable dinner-parties at night. In this hectic atmosphere family life naturally suffered. Women gained greater economic independence, divorce became more common, and immorality increased. But while the wild life of a fashionable set around Clodia might make headline news, many men lived moderate and cultured lives. The nobles continued to draw their wealth from their large estates and from the profits of provincial administration. Not less wealthy in many cases were the Equites, who, debarred from politics, built up wide financial undertakings: they helped the government to collect the provincial taxes, and as individuals or as organised companies they engaged in industry, commerce, banking, and money-lending throughout the Roman world. They provided the essential machinery for the economic development of the Empire. But as standards of morality fell, many *publicani* began callously to exploit the unfortunate provincials. Together the senatorial and equestrian orders represented the upper class at Rome, although they were separated by a political and to some extent by a social gulf. Their mutual relations were more often than not hostile; and this breach, which Cicero's efforts failed to heal, was one factor that helped to bring about the collapse of the Republic.

The rest of the city population consisted of many groups. There were the clients of the nobles and Equites who were established by their patrons in various pursuits; the self-supporting small business-men, shopkeepers, and workmen, many of whom were freedmen or sons of freedmen; the urban proletariat which relied on the corn dole and lived in squalor in blocks of high tenements (*insulae*); resident foreigners; and great numbers of slaves, who served in the houses of the rich or in trade and industry, as well as working on the land. Many of these slaves were foreigners, especially Greeks and Easterners, and were often better educated than their Roman masters, whom they might serve as doctors or teachers. Since the Romans were generous in freeing slaves, the freedman element in the population was high; and this meant that the old Italian population was being steadily adulterated in a city that was soon to number not much less than a million inhabitants. Further, the demand by the urban population for free food and entertainment (*panem et circenses*) increased, and many of the public entertainments were brutal and degrading: besides chariot racing, animal fights and gladiatorial combats in the arena excited the blood-lust of the crowds. But alongside such revolting cruelty and the sufferings of slaves who worked in gangs on the plantations or in the mines, no doubt throughout a large part of the countryside of Italy, life in fields and farms went on much as usual and older standards of family life and honest toil prevailed.

Despite civil war and frequent devastation or confiscation of land, Italy remained prosperous. It included all Cisalpine Gaul after Caesar had extended citizen rights to the Transpadanes, and not only had it been politically united after the Social War but Roman culture and ways of life tended to spread more widely throughout it. Its industrial and commercial life developed on traditional lines, and the prosperity of its towns is illustrated by the growth of Pompeii. Further, Italian business-men settled in considerable numbers in the provinces, acquiring land there and exploiting their economic possibilities. The standard of provincial government declined; and while not all suffered the excesses of maladministration that Sicily did under Verres, there was much oppression and exploitation.

Roman culture at this time was a blend of Greek and Roman traditions, and the Greece that inspired the Romans was not only that of the classical age but no less that of the later Hellenistic world. Sculptors and architects turned for inspiration to cities like Pergamum and Alexandria; Latin poets admired Alexandrian poetry; and Cicero owed as much to the philosopher Poseidonius (ca. 135–50 B.C.) as to Plato. Rome's debt to Greece was perhaps greatest in art, and in the late Republic there was an astonishing demand for copies of great originals, though the Romans made their own contribution, not least in portraiture. In architecture too they learned much, but they infused what they borrowed with their own spirit. Throughout Italy and the Roman world Roman buildings were constantly being constructed: temples, basilicas, bridges, aqueducts, drains, triumphal arches, city walls, tombs, baths, theatres, amphitheatres, town and country houses; while Rome owed to the genius of its engineers those thousands of miles of roads that linked its world together and promoted its economic and administrative life.

The Ciceronian age saw the flowering of much fine literature. This included the work of two great poets. Lucretius wrote a poem on the nature of the universe, in which he expounded the views of Epicurus, including his materialistic view of life which he believed would free men from superstition and fear of death. Although his theme was didactic, his poetry reached great heights of splendour. Catullus wrote short lyrics on a variety of subjects of a freshness and sincerity that was hitherto quite unknown in Roman poetry. Other writers turned to history, oratory, and philosophy. Sallust for political purposes wrote monographs on Jugurtha and Catiline as well as general history, while Caesar's *Commentaries* on his Gallic and Civil Wars provide a classic example of vigorous and lucid exposition. In Cicero Roman oratory reached its highest point, while his letters throw a fascinating light on the man and his times. Not least of his contributions were his philosophical works, in which he tried to popularise Greek thought for Roman readers. He himself steered a middle course between the claims of Stoics and Epicureans; both these creeds, and especially the former, were gaining ever more adherents among educated Romans. The tastes of those who wanted a different approach to life were catered for by the spread of astrology and of many more Eastern cults, such as those of Cybele or Isis.

THE AUGUSTAN AGE

After his victory at Actium in 31 B.C. Octavian was the undisputed master of the Roman world. He faced a situation which had arisen from the breakdown of senatorial government and the rise of military commanders. Could he restore the former and control the latter? To give up his own power would result in fresh civil war, while to hold it as a military dictator would be to risk Caesar's fate. He must try to make the old constitution work, and yet he must retain his unified military command not only to secure internal peace but also to protect the frontiers of the Empire. By trial and error he reached a solution that was so satisfactory that it gave the world a stable government for the next two centuries.

He skilfully guided Rome from war to peace. In 27 B.C., when he was given the name Augustus and the title *Princeps Civitatis*, he surrendered his powers only to receive back from the Senate the administration of many of the provinces. Officially the Republic was restored, with Augustus as its chief magistrate. In fact constitutional government was restored, with the Princeps as virtually a constitutional monarch. After further adjustments in 23 B.C. his civil authority rested on a grant of tribunician power and his military authority on a grant of proconsular *imperium* that was greater than that of any other proconsul. No less delicate than his own position was the problem of his relations with the Senate. He decided that he would share with it the work of administering the Empire, but ultimate power he could not share: he remained the commander of the army and retained the loyalty of the legions. At home the Senate's functions were even increased. It could now pass laws, and not merely recommend them to the people; the rôle of the people in the state gradually almost disappeared. The Senate could also act as a high court of justice, continued to control the Treasury (*Aerarium*), and administered Rome, Italy, and the peaceful provinces. Parallel with it Augustus had powers of legislation, jurisdiction, finance, and the administration of the frontier provinces where armies might be needed.

In order to provide an adequate supply of officials (one cause of the collapse of the Republic had been the lack of a civil service), Augustus laid down strict measures to limit entry into the senatorial and equestrian orders to those who were properly qualified. Men from these orders

172. The Arch of Titus at Rome, erected to commemorate the capture of Jerusalem, as seen from the Colosseum. Left, the Palatine; in the background, the Capitoline. 173. The Arch of Trajan at Benevento records Trajan's victories. 174. The triumphant Emperor is the subject of many reliefs: the goddess Victoria places a victor's crown on Trajan's head. 175. Many Emperors were not only administrators and conquerors but also builders: fragment of scene showing Trajan during sacrifice before a bridge built by his troops. 176. Impressive remains of Trajan's defence system still dot the Syrian desert: fort at Palmyra. 177. At Tivoli Hadrian built a magnificent villa, of which some imposing ruins still remain. 178. This Emperor also built a defence wall on the frontier of Britain when native tribes threatened the security of the border areas.

172

174

5

6

177

178

179

180

181

182

183

184

185

186

187

could then proceed upon public careers, the stages of which were carefully graded; they became professional administrators, replacing the amateurs of the Republic. In like manner also the army became professional. Augustus established a standing army of some 28 legions, recruited from Roman citizens, and a like number of auxiliary troops (*Auxilia*), who received citizenship on discharge after twenty-five years' service. The troops were stationed in permanent camps in the frontier provinces to guard the Empire. Augustus also created a crack corps, the Praetorian Guard, in Italy. To maintain order in Rome three Urban Cohorts were established, while seven cohorts of Watchmen (*Vigiles*) guarded against fire. Thus Augustus tried to ensure the maintenance of order both at home and throughout the Roman world.

It was little use to devise good machinery for the state if the men who worked it were corrupt or inefficient. Augustus therefore planned a series of social reforms aimed at improving the morals and conduct of the governing class in particular. Laws were passed to encourage marriage, family life, and the birth-rate, to make adultery a public crime, and to discourage divorce. Since Augustus laid much emphasis on the old Roman and Italian traditions (in contrast to Antony's leanings to Eastern ideas), he wished to restrict the dilution of the Italian stock that had resulted from its interpenetration by freedmen, who were often of Eastern origin. He therefore made manumission of slaves more difficult. Thus his policy of extending Roman citizenship was less generous than the normal Roman attitude. He tried to curb luxury, and lived a simple life himself. To encourage moral regeneration he directed attention to Rome's earlier and simpler ways of life, particularly in the sphere of religion. He suppressed foreign cults and encouraged the revival of many old cults, building or restoring some eighty temples. He discouraged any attempt at emperor

179. The only classical equestrian statue to survive is that of Marcus Aurelius. 180. The pedestal of a monument in honour of Antoninus Pius shows a parade of infantry and cavalry. 181. The Emperor Septimius Severus introduces Caracalla to the Senate. 182. It was a sign of the turning tide when Aurelian built a wall round Rome: the wall where the Via Appia enters. 183. Diocletian succeeded in reorganising the Empire and halting, though only temporarily, the approaching decline. 184. The history of pagan Rome ended with the accession of Constantine the Great, who recognised Christianity as the state religion. 185. Triumphal arch erected after his victory at Pons Milvius. 186. The remains of Imperial Rome make it possible to visualise the capital. The greatest monument is the Flavian amphitheatre, the Colosseum (see reconstruction in (218). 187. Relief probably showing the Via Sacra.

worship in Rome, but in the East, where men had long been accustomed to worship their rulers, he allowed a cult of 'Roma et Augustus', believing that this would prove a useful bond of unity between the Princeps and the provinces.

At home his efforts were supported by three great writers. Livy wrote a history of Rome from earliest times on a vast scale (in 142 Books, of which less than one-quarter survive), in which he emphasised the *mos maiorum* and the moral qualities that had made Rome great; it was a pageant of the past, designed to inspire Livy's own generation. Horace wrote lyric poems of great charm and consummate workmanship, as well as Satires, and in his so-called Roman Odes (the first six poems of his third Book) he too gave fine expression to the traditional virtues of the race. Lastly, Virgil during the civil war had composed his *Georgics*, which not only gave advice to farmers but also showed the deep satisfaction that a man may gain from honest labour on his native soil. Encouraged by Augustus, Virgil composed an epic poem. In the *Aeneid* he adopted the legend that Rome's origins went back to the Trojan hero Aeneas, and in this national epic he unfolded the source and heritage of his countrymen. The splendid and sonorous hexameters are filled with pride in Rome's past, faith in the peoples of Italy, and confidence in their future; but the strong belief in Rome's imperial mission is matched by a profound feeling for the suffering of mankind. He raised the Latin language to such a pinnacle of expressive and poetic perfection that his work has remained to this day the type and symbol of a 'classic'; and his was one of the few names from antiquity to live (in the strangely distorted guise of a powerful magician) through the Dark Ages when almost all else was forgotten. The frivolous love poems of Ovid were less in tune with the aims of Augustus, so that it is not surprising that when the poet became involved in a private scandal the Emperor banished him from Rome. Thus Augustus and his friends tried to regenerate Roman society and stir men afresh to their responsibilities.

To signify the dawn of this new era, the Secular Games were celebrated in 17 B.C., for which Horace composed a Processional Hymn (*Carmen Saeculare*), while the restoration of peace found expression in the erection in 13 B.C. of the Ara Pacis on the Campus Martius, one of the great monuments of the Augustan age. Further, Rome must be made a worthy capital of the Empire, in a physical as well as a moral sense. Therefore Augustus promoted a great building scheme: 'He found Rome brick and left it marble.' In the centre of his new Forum arose the temple of Mars Ultor, vowed at Philippi; other buildings included a temple to Apollo on the Palatine, a portico in honour of his sister Octavia, a theatre in memory of his nephew Marcellus, and the Pantheon, which was the responsibility of his friend Agrippa to whom he owed much in war and peace.

To safeguard the Empire Augustus had to face the difficult problems of fixing and securing its frontiers. These must be pushed well back from the heart of the Empire, but distant frontiers meant entrusting armies

Exposed view of the Ara Pacis of Augustus, erected in 9 B.C. in honour of the Emperor.

to men far from the Emperor's direct supervision, and long frontiers in-volved more men and expense. Augustus tried therefore to establish as economical a frontier system as was consistent with safety, and then laid down as a maxim to his successors that they should keep the Empire within the boundaries that he had provided for it. The peaceful provinces would continue to be the responsibility of the Senate, and their governors were called proconsuls (even if they had previously held only the praetor-ship). The Imperial provinces were administered by deputies of the Emperor who, whether ex-praetors or ex-consuls, were called *legati Augusti pro praetore*, while very small Imperial provinces (such as Judaea) were governed by procurators of equestrian, and not senatorial, rank.

In the East beyond the Euphrates was the Parthian Empire which might challenge Rome for control of at least Asia Minor and which had defeated

Roman armies under Crassus and Antony. Augustus might well have launched a war of revenge such as Julius Caesar had contemplated, but instead he managed by diplomatic means to negotiate a settlement under which Rome received back the captured standards of the legions that the Parthians had overwhelmed. He counted this an important success, and no serious trouble with Parthia developed until the reign of Nero. As a precaution, however, Augustus reorganised the client kingdoms in Asia and annexed Galatia as a province on the death of its king in 25 B.C. Farther south there was trouble in Judaea after the death in 4 B.C. of King Herod the Great. After ten years of misrule by one of his sons Judaea was made a province in A.D. 6. Augustus had annexed Egypt after the defeat of Antony and Cleopatra; it did not become a normal province but remained under the Emperor's direct authority and was administered for him by a Prefect of equestrian, not senatorial, rank. Certain adjustments were made in Africa, and Spain was finally pacified. Augustus himself and Agrippa campaigned against the Cantabrians of the northwest, and the peninsula was divided into three provinces: Tarraconensis, Baetica, and Lusitania. Gaul also was reorganised as four provinces: Narbonensis, Aquitania, Lugdunensis, and Belgica.

The main danger point seemed to Augustus to lie on the northern frontier beyond the Alps and the Balkans. Here he decided upon radical change – to advance the frontier as far as the Danube. In a series of campaigns, in which his two stepsons, Tiberius and Drusus, took a leading part, this aim was gradually accomplished. The country south of the western part of the Danube was reduced by about 15 B.C. and turned into two provinces, Raetia (eastern Switzerland and the Tyrol) and Noricum (roughly Austria). Farther east the Pannonians (western Hungary) and the Dalmatians (western Yugoslavia) were defeated, and after a great revolt in A.D. 6 they were pacified. Pannonia was made a province, as also was Moesia to the east, but Thrace was left under a client king. Thus the Empire was now advanced to the whole length of the Danube. The western flank of the Danube line was covered by Roman control of the Rhine; but Augustus decided that it would be both safer and more economical if the frontier was advanced eastwards over the Rhine to the Elbe and then joined up through the land of the Marcomanni (Bohemia) to the Danube. The advance was made to the Elbe, but the revolt of Pannonia delayed the attempt to reduce the Marcomanni. The Romans suffered another terrible setback in A.D. 9, when a general, Varus, with three legions was annihilated in the Teutobergian Forest in western Germany. This so dismayed the elderly Augustus that he decided to fall back on the Rhine-Danube frontier and to abandon any attempt to hold ground east of the Rhine. Instead no less than eight legions were permanently stationed in six camps along the length of the Rhine.

Problems of frontier defence were not the only anxieties that engaged Augustus' attention. The whole security of the Empire might be threatened if he died without having made arrangements for the future that would be acceptable to the Senate and still more to the army. His trouble was that he had no son, only a daugther, whom he used as a pawn in his dynastic plans. These cannot be traced here, beyond noting that he was dogged by extraordinary ill-luck. Various possible successors died: his nephew Marcellus, his friend Agrippa, his stepson Drusus, and his two grandsons, Gaius and Lucius Caesar. At last he was forced to turn to his other stepson Tiberius, whom because of his character he did not regard as very suitable. However, he adopted Tiberius as his son in A.D. 4, and in 13 Tiberius received such powers that he was virtually co-regent. In theory there was no problem: when the Princeps died the Senate and people (*senatus populusque Romanus*) had to decide if they wanted a new Princeps or whether the old Republic should function again. But, as Augustus knew full well, in practice this was impossible, and the only way to avert civil war was to raise someone to a position which in fact could not be challenged. Not the least of the debts which Rome owed to Augustus was that he secured that the peace which he had given the Roman world was not shattered when he died in A.D. 14.

THE EARLY EMPIRE (TO A.D. 193)

Fortunately for the peace of the world, Tiberius was an experienced soldier and administrator who, despite an embittered character, was determined to rule with firmness and efficiency. One of the tragedies of his principate was that he was unable to maintain such co-operation with the Senate as Augustus had enjoyed, and their relations gradually deteriorated as time went by. The first nine years of his reign were a period of efficient administration, but after the death of his son Drusus in A.D. 23 he increasingly relied on his friend Sejanus whom he had made Prefect of the Praetorian Guard. As the Guard was now stationed in Rome, its commander had great power, and Sejanus plotted to overthrow the unsuspecting

Tiberius. The plot was unmasked in 31. But the discovery of his supposed friend's treachery so changed Tiberius that he developed into a suspicious tyrant, and the last six years of his rule saw a reign of terror in which informers flourished and treason trials increased. Nevertheless, provincial administration continued to be good, and few changes were made, except that Cappadocia was annexed as a province.

Lacking a son, Tiberius had adopted his grand-nephew Gaius (Caligula), who succeeded without difficulty in A.D. 37. Although this young man started well, he soon became mentally unbalanced, or at any rate power went to his head and he became a bloodthirsty tyrant. Luckily for Rome he was murdered in 41 in a conspiracy in which the Praetorians had played a major part. The Guard now took the initiative: while the Senate was debating what should be done, it turned to Gaius' uncle, Claudius, and forced the Senate to accept him as Emperor. This nephew of Tiberius had been kept in the background during his fifty years; but although not very personable he had considerable intelligence and a deep understanding of Rome's past. In the surviving literary tradition he is depicted as the weak tool of his wives and freedmen servants; but in fact he showed considerable individuality in the exercise of power. In order to increase administrative efficiency he built up the civil service by developing five special departments or 'ministries', each under a freedman head. Some of these freedmen became very rich and powerful and gave great offence to the senators on whose sphere of adminstration Claudius and his servants tended to encroach, despite the fact that the Emperor made sincere efforts to co-operate with the Senate. Claudius felt that the time had come for fresh developments in the Imperial field. He gave Roman citizenship to provincials much more freely than his predecessors had done, and he incorporated no less than five new provinces in the Empire. These were Mauretania (two provinces), Thrace, Lycia, and Britain. He himself went to Britain in 43 after his expeditionary force had gained a footing. The southeast was made into a province, from which Roman armies were to advance to further conquest, and a colony of veterans was settled at Camulodunum (Colchester). In his domestic affairs Claudius was less successful, and although he had a son of his own, Britannicus, he was persuaded by his fourth wife Agrippina to adopt her son by a previous marriage, Nero. He died in 54, quite possibly poisoned by Agrippina, and power passed smoothly to Agrippina's sixteen-year-old son, who was a great-great-grandson of Augustus.

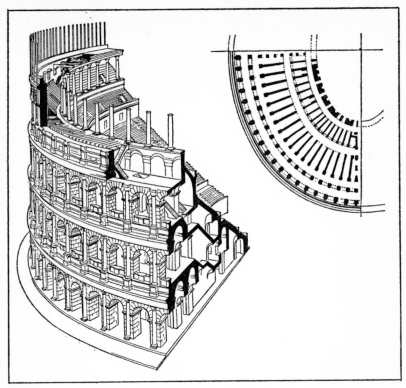

Segment and plan of the Amphitheatrum Flavium (Colosseum) in Rome (A.D. 80).

As long as Nero was willing to follow the advice of his tutor Seneca and of the Praetorian Prefect Burrus, the government went on quietly. But before long Nero wanted to be undisputed master. He murdered Britannicus and his own mother Agrippina, he dismissed Seneca, and then had his own wife Octavia killed in order that he might marry Poppaea. In 64 a financial crisis was followed by a great fire that gutted a large part of Rome. To divert from himself the increasing hatred of the people, Nero blamed the new sect of Christians for the fire, and the first persecution took place. But while Nero indulged his artistic leanings and did not hesitate to appear in public as singer or charioteer, conspiracies arose, although that led by Piso in 65 was crushed. There was also discontent abroad. Nero had tried to annex Armenia, and this had resulted in a military defeat by the Parthians at Rhandeia, although an agreement was finally reached with them. In Britain Boudicca (Boadicea) had led the Iceni in revolt and been crushed. In 66 a great revolt flared up in Palestine. When discontent spread to the armies Nero's fate was sealed. Vindex, governor of Gallia Lugdunensis, revolted but was soon crushed. Galba in Spain followed suit, and with him Otho, governor of Lusitania. Deserted by the Praetorians and declared a public enemy by the Senate, Nero was forced to commit suicide (68).

With Nero's death a new situation arose. He and his predecessors (the Julio-Claudians) had all been linked with the Imperial family; but now there was no such potential successor. The fate of Rome rested in the hands of the army commanders, and 'a secret was revealed, that an Emperor could be made elsewhere than at Rome'. The succession could only be decided by force of arms. Civil war followed, and the whole system that Augustus had created was in jeopardy. The year 69 was the 'year of the four emperors'. Galba was soon overthrown by Otho, who was backed by the legions on the Danube and in Syria; but the Rhine armies successfully claimed the throne for their commander Vitellius. The Danubian and Eastern legions, however, put forward Vespasian, who was conducting the Jewish war, which he left to his son Titus to complete while he himself went to Rome.

It was Rome's good fortune that Vespasian was of very different temperament from Nero. He was of Sabine stock, hard-headed and practical, a man of comparatively simple tastes. He also had two sons, a fact which might help to avert civil war when he died. He thus appeared as a new founder of the Empire, to which he restored peace and order. At home he exercised economy, encouraged a simpler court life, and chose his public servants on their merits rather than because of their birth: it was in 80 that the first African reached the consulship. In the East, where Titus had destroyed Jerusalem in 70, Vespasian strengthened and enlarged Gala-

188. The heart of Rome was the Forum Romanum, where remains of temples and other buildings still reflect the impressive character of the ancient city. In the background, the Capitoline and the Tabularium, with the Arch of Septimius Severus in front; left, the Palatine. 189. Their excellent road system was one reason why the Romans managed to retain power for such a long time: the Fosse Way in England, still an important highway. 190. At Portus Adurni, now Portchester, the square Roman fort, with its walls and towers, still stands. 191. Roman fortress built within an earlier native earthwork: Hod Hill in Dorset. 192. At Silchester the outlines of the walled town and its street plan can still be seen from lines in the fields. 193. Where declining authority brought danger to frontiers, extensive walls and other defence works were constructed. Hadrian's Wall in northern Britain.

90

91

192

193

194

195

198

199

200

201

tia and Syria. In Britain the Brigantes in the north and the Silures in southern Wales were reduced, while the Rhine frontier, which had been threatened by a serious revolt in 69, was strengthened by the annexation of the Black Forest area (Agri Decumates). When Vespasian died peacefully in 79, his popular son Titus succeeded without a hitch, but died from fever two years later. His reign was noteworthy for the eruption of Vesuvius and the opening of the Amphitheatrum Flavium or Colosseum. He was followed by his younger brother Domitian, whose rule was much harsher.

Cruel by nature, Domitian developed into a suspicious tyrant after the rebellion in 88 of the commander of the army of Upper Germany. But his hatred was directed chiefly against the senatorial and upper classes, while the people and legionaries were mainly contented, and the administration remained good. Some extensions were made in the provinces. In Britain Agricola advanced successfully into Caledonia. On the Rhine the frontier was moved forward to include the Taunus district, and the Rhineland was constituted as the two provinces of Upper and Lower Germany. Farther east, the Dacians (in Romania) had burst over the Danube into Moesia, but were defeated by 89, and Moesia was divided into two provinces. Thus both at home and abroad these three Flavian Emperors served Rome well, but at a certain cost: the powers of the Princeps had steadily increased. Unlike Augustus, who after 23 B.C. had avoided the consulship and declined the censorship, Domitian held the consulship frequently and became *censor perpetuus*. The Imperial cult also developed, and Domitian welcomed, if he did not demand, such appellations as *dominus* and even *deus*. Further, the Senate was now dominated by the Emperor, although its members, who were increasingly drawn from the municipal aristocracies and provincials, were more representative of the Empire. But if the Emperor was more absolute, he was also regarded

194. The ruins at modern Timgad in Algeria give a clear idea of the layout of a Roman town: square, with straight streets intersecting at right angles; it was designed on camp lines. 198. Remains, including arches, of Roman baths at Volubilis in Mauretania. 196. Lambaesis in Algeria was a fortified camp. 197. Triumphal arch and other ruins at Volubilis. 195. The Roman navy had several bases in the Mediterranean, the main one being at Cape Misenum near Naples. These bases, the road network, and the system of army camps made extensive trade and travel safe and possible under the Pax Romana. 199. Travel scene from Gaul. 200. Mosaics, reliefs, etc., still bear witness to the considerable traffic between provinces. Mosaic, in Ostia, of a Roman merchant ship; top left, a lighthouse. 201. Transhipment of amphoras.

as a kind of earthly providence. Thus Rome owed the Flavian dynasty a great debt: peace and orderly government were re-established, and confidence in Rome's future was restored.

When Domitian was murdered in 96 risk of civil war was averted through the tact of a senior senator named Nerva whom the Senate chose to succeed him. Nerva, who was liberal in temper and policy, laid the foundations for the prosperity of the next hundred years, under the so-called 'five good emperors', by securing the orderly continuation of government. As he had no sons, he adopted and made co-regent a man whom the army would support, Marcus Ulpius Traianus, then commander in Upper Germany. Thus when Nerva died two years later (98) power passed to Trajan without difficulty. Although his authority was no less than that of Domitian, he exercised it in a very different spirit. He showed such forbearance to the Senate that it conferred upon him with real gratitude the title of Optimus. He devoted much attention to the well-being of Rome and Italy, instituting relief schemes for poor children (*alimenta*), encouraging agriculture, spending lavishly on public buildings (such as his Forum) and games. But he was first of all a soldier, and he believed that the time had come to take drastic action to protect the northern and eastern frontiers by further conquest and annexation. After two wars against Decebalus, king of the Dacians, Trajan made Dacia a Roman province, thus advancing the Empire beyond the Danube (106). So thoroughly did this area become Romanised that it still bears the name Romania. His Eastern policy was less wise. Arabia Petraea, the district around the caravan city of Petra, was annexed in 106, but before long Trajan determined to try conclusions with the Parthians. In a series of campaigns (113–16) he defeated them and advanced to the Persian Gulf, having added Armenia, Mesopotamia, and Assyria to the Roman Empire. But a Parthian counter-attack in his rear, a widespread Jewish revolt in the Levant, and failing health, led him to return home, leaving Hadrian in command in Syria. On the journey he died in Cilicia (117), having indicated Hadrian as his successor.

Hadrian continued Trajan's policy of co-operation with the Senate, but in many ways he encroached upon senatorial prerogatives. He reorganised and gave greater responsibilities to the equestrian order, both as members of an Imperial Council and in the Imperial civil service (where Equites replaced freedmen). Like his predecessor he showed concern for public works both at home and in the provinces, while his reign was marked by some notable developments in the field of law. His versatile character led him to take a personal interest in the Empire as a whole and to travel extensively on long tours of inspection. His foreign policy differed from that of Trajan. Although he retained Dacia, he decided to abandon Trajan's eastern conquests, and allowed Mesopotamia and Assyria to revert to Parthian control. While diplomacy largely replaced war, Hadrian did much

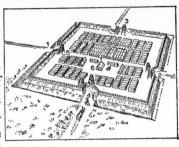

Roman camp (*castra*). 1. Main gate; 2. Right gate; 3. Praetorian gate; 4. Decuman gate; 5. Main way; 6. Praetorium.

to strengthen the army and to develop a protective frontier system for the Empire. In the Rhineland, defences were strengthened, forts often being built of stone instead of earth; but his best-known work is in northern Britain. Here Agricola's Scottish conquests had been abandoned early in Trajan's reign, and Hadrian built a frontier wall for eighty miles across the island. But he could not avoid all fighting. A great Jewish revolt in 132 and its supression laid the country in ruins. Jews were forbidden to visit Jerusalem (now Aelia Capitolina), and Judaea was renamed Syria Palestina. Since he had no children, Hadrian made elaborate plans for the succession, so that when he died in 138 power passed easily to his adopted son, Antoninus Pius.

Under Antoninus Pius (138–61) the Empire enjoyed one of its most secure periods, an Indian Summer that Gibbon regarded as the happiest era known to man. His administration reflected his industrious and kindly nature, though the concern of the central government was beginning to develop into paternalism, with the consequent weakening of local self-government. His successor Marcus Aurelius (161–80), who was a Stoic philosopher of high ideals, followed a similar policy. In order to facilitate his task he conferred the title of Augustus on his adoptive brother, L. Verus; this nominal joint rule, which ended with Verus' death in 169, foreshadows the division of Imperial power. But difficulties gradually increased. A devastating plague from the East inflicted widespread losses, and barbarians threatened the frontiers. Antoninus had built a wall in Scotland and an advance fortified line east of the Rhine and Danube in an attempt to strengthen the weak spots. Marcus Aurelius, although a man of peace, had to make war for sixteen of the nineteen years of his rule. Fresh action had to be taken against the Parthians, while a greater danger arose when Germanic tribes (Marcomanni and Quadi) invaded the Danubian provinces and even raided Italy itself. In a long series of campaigns Marcus repelled the danger, and he then planned to advance the frontier to the Carpathians and the mountains of Bohemia; but after his death his successor abandoned this plan. Since the death of Domitian the succession had been secured by adoption and the 'choice of the best'; but Marcus had a son Commodus, to whose vices he was too indulgent. Family affection led him to choose his son as successor. This reversion to the dynastic principle was not well conceived. Commodus' rule (180–93) was weak and corrupt; the moral basis on which recent Emperors had set the Principate was undermined; and the way was made ready for the Dominate, when the Emperor was Lord and when the military triumphed over the civilian conception of the Principate.

LIFE UNDER THE EMPIRE

'The boundless majesty of the Roman peace' (*immensa Romanae pacis maiestas*) enabled the Roman Empire to attain its highest point of economic development. It was a vast area bound together in one system, stretching from Scotland to the Sahara, from Spain to the Euphrates, some 1,600 miles the one way and 2,800 the other. Rome had made no effort to impose any uniformity of culture throughout the Empire, but allowed the provincials to retain their varied customs and institutions, under the aegis of Roman law and justice. Thus many languages continued to be spoken, such as Celtic in Gaul and Britain, Punic in Africa, and Aramaic in Syria; but two languages predominated, Latin in the West and Greek in the East. Similarly the predominantly Latin culture of the West was complementary to the Hellenism of the East.

In general there was economic, racial, and religious toleration. There were no frontiers or serious customs barriers to hinder the world-wide exchange of goods; there was no colour bar; and men were free to worship whatever gods they wished (only three religions, Druidism, Judaism, and Christianity, provoked persecution by the Imperial government, the first because it involved human sacrifice, the other two because of their monotheistic claims). It is true that the culture of the Empire meant less to the masses in the provinces than to the upper and middle classes

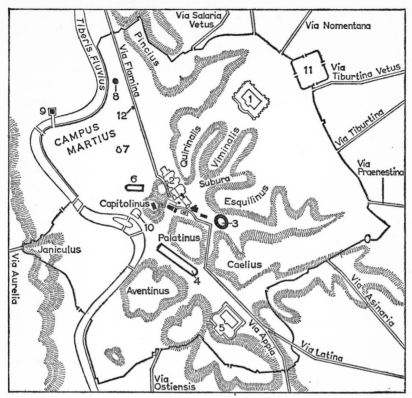

Rome under the Empire. 1. Baths of Diocletian; 2. Forums; 3. Colosseum; 4. Circus Maximus; 5. Baths of Caracalla; 6. Circus Flaminius; 7. Pantheon; 8. Mausoleum of Augustus; 9. Mausoleum of Hadrian; 10. Theatre of Marcellus; 11. Praetorian camp; 12. Ara Pacis.

whom the Empire chiefly benefited, and that no real attempt was made to deal with such social evils as slavery or the pauperisation of urban populations, or to secure adequate provincial representation in the managing of affairs. True also, Rome might fall short of its general good standards in some cases, such as its relations with the Jews, while a natural hatred of Rome would burn, at any rate at first, in the hearts of those free tribesmen beyond the frontiers of the Empire whom Rome forced to come within. Nevertheless many of the barriers between a privileged Italy and subject provinces had fallen; provinces could more easily voice any grievances (through provincial Councils); and by the age of the Antonines government was more humane in spirit than in earlier days. Further, despite the great diversities throughout the Empire, there was a real feeling of unity, and men looked to their Princeps as to a universal providence by whose personal interest and care the Roman Peace was preserved.

Control of the Empire by the central government was achieved not merely through the larger provincial units, but essentially by its relations with the individual cities, which retained a very high degree of self-government. In the East the Greek institution of the city-state was of long standing and widespread; in the West, where cities were fewer, Rome encouraged and promoted their growth. These smaller units, in which men spent their lives, could more easily attract their devotion and patriotism. Throughout the provinces urbanisation reached its widest extent. Under local aristocracies of public-spirited men, who often spent generously to endow and maintain their own cities, the municipalities flourished and sought to outshine each other. The care which the Emperors lavished on cities and provinces is illustrated by the correspondence between Trajan and Pliny while the latter was administering Bithynia, or by Hadrian's tours of inspection. Since Trajan and his three successors were of Spanish or Gallic origin, they were naturally liberal in their grants of Roman citizenship to provincials. The outward appearance also of the cities improved: everywhere forums, theatres, amphitheatres, baths, aqueducts, and bridges provided greater facilities. Sometimes local financial difficulties or inefficiency might lead the central government to intervene to give help. This tendency, which developed in the second century unfortunately increased in the third with disastrous results, so that ultimately local political life and self-government withered away under the oppressive burden of bureaucratic control.

The city was the pre-eminent channel for the diffusion of culture, but agriculture remained the basis of economic life throughout Italy and the provinces. There was a tendency for the ownership of land to be concentrated in fewer hands, and the Emperor himself became the greatest landowner; but many small or moderate estates still flourished in Italy. Industry and commerce increased, and the provinces competed successfully with Italy. Peace by land and sea, and the improvement of communications, especially the roads, naturally promoted the interchange of goods, and there was a vast and constant flow of raw materials and manufactured articles through the length and breadth of the Empire. Nor did it stop there. Commerce extended beyond the bounds of the Empire to East Africa, Arabia, southern India, and beyond, while by land luxury goods came from China through Afghanistan. No passports were needed, and men could travel freely throughout the Empire: if a Syrian or Asiatic craftsman or merchant thought that prospects were brighter in Rome or the Western provinces, he might migrate and settle there. Freedom of travel is well illustrated in the journeys made by St Paul in the eastern Mediterranean, although he had the additional benefit, enjoyed by more and more men as time went on, of Roman citizenship.

The prosperity of the cities, however, was won at the expense of the country. Economically these were largely parasitic, and the standard

Reconstruction of the Basilica of Trajan at Rome (ca. A.D. 110)

of living for peasants might be lower even than that of an urban proletariat. There were extremes of wealth and poverty, from the local municipal millionaire to the wretched slave in the mine; but something was done in the second century to alleviate some of the worst evils of poverty and slavery by public and private benevolence and by Imperial legislation. Nowhere were the contrasts more marked than in Rome itself. With a population of nearly a million inhabitants, it was enriched by successive Emperors with ever more magnificent buildings, while the poor lived in slums and squalor. But it had a different population from earlier days, not only racially more mixed but also morally less robust: the satirist Juvenal observed that 'the people that once bestowed commands, consulships, legions, and all else, now meddles no more and eagerly longs for just two things, bread and circuses'. The spoilt population demanded regular free distributions of corn (*frumentationes*) and expected the Emperor on occasion to make gifts of money (*congiaria*). Even as early as Claudius' reign there were 159 holidays a year in the Roman calendar, on 93 of which games were given at public expense. There were theatres for acting, stadia for athletics, circuses for chariot racing, and amphitheatres for gladiatorial and animal contests. These last throw a dark shadow on the life of the Romans, who had little respect for human life and in whom there had always been a streak of cruelty or at least indifference to suffering.

Not all men, however, found relaxation in such ways. The 'golden' age of Augustan literature was followed by a period of 'silver'. As autocracy increased, freedom of expression tended to be circumscribed, while literature suffered still more from the stifling effects of rhetoric. Rhetorical training was not only a regular method of instruction in schools, but declamation became a popular social activity and authors commonly recited their works to an audience before publication. This might lead in literature to mere verbal dexterity and epigrammatic effect, which was often more artificial than brilliant, although some writers of Silver Latin touched greatness. The tragedies of Seneca have exercised an influence on European literature out of proportion to their literary merits. Lucan in his *Pharsalia* described in epic form the civil war between Caesar and Pompey, while Martial's epigrams cast a vivid light on Rome under Domitian. The greatest and most powerful of the poets was Juvenal from Aquinum (ca. 50–127), whose satires burn with fierce indignation at human folly. Among prose writers one of the most interesting is Petronius, who lived under Nero and wrote a novel about the adventures of three disreputable young men in southern Italy. The *Natural History* of the Elder Pliny, who perished during the eruption of Vesuvius in 79, is a work of encyclopaedic

202. As early as the Republican era Roman domestic architecture reached a high standard. The House of the Masks in Delos shows the layout of a Hellenistic-Roman house built round an inner court. 203–4. Ruins indicate the size and decoration of the houses. Remains of flats at Ostia. 205. Ruins of a block of flats at Ostia. 206. Reconstruction of the dwelling-house whose remains are shown in 205. Houses and villas of prominent Romans were enriched with mosaics, frescoes, etc. 207. Mosaic from the House of Masks (see 202), ca. 100 B.C., showing Dionysus riding on a panther. 208. Floral still-life from Pompeii. 209. A much depicted event in Roman life is the marriage ceremony; it consisted in the joining of right hands. 210. Husband and wife at a meal, another frequently represented scene.

202

203

207

208

209

210

211

212

213

214

215

216

217

218

219

220

learning, while his nephew the Younger Pliny published ten books of *Epistles*, including his reports as governor of Bithynia and the replies of Trajan. But the greatest writer of the age is the historian Tacitus, who in addition to monographs on his father-in-law Agricola and on Germany wrote the history of Rome from Tiberius to Nero (the *Annals*) and of the years 69–96 in the *Histories*. These powerful and dramatic works are the glory of Silver Latin literature. Of a very different calibre, but of great interest, are the *Lives of the Twelve Caesars* by Suetonius (ca. 69–140). Two writers of African origin belong to a slightly later time: Fronto, whose correspondence with his pupil Marcus Aurelius survives, and Apuleius, whose *Metamorphoses* or *Golden Ass* is a novel concerned with the mysteries of Isis. Nor should the contribution of Greek writers be forgotten: Plutarch's *Lives of Greeks and Romans*, Josephus' account of the Jewish War, Lucian's humorous dialogues, and the speeches of Aelius Aristeides (including a eulogy of Rome) and of Dio Chrysostom; slightly later come the Roman histories of Appian and Dio Cassius. Many more technical works were also produced. Vitruvius wrote in Latin on architecture, Celsus and Galen on medicine, Columela on agriculture, and Ptolemy on astronomy and geography.

Little original work was produced in philosophy, but the philosophic schools flourished at Athens, Alexandria, and elsewhere. Epicureanism might lose its influence, but there was a revival of Cynicism, and the great influence of Stoicism was extended by the writings of the ex-slave Epictetus and by the *Meditations* of Marcus Aurelius, in whose person a Stoic philosopher became ruler. More popular interest was aroused by extreme Cynic beggars and the itinerant teachers of the so-called Second Sophistic movement. The third century saw the last great development of classical philosophy, the mystical interpretation of Plato by Plotinus,

Reliefs give many details of daily life. **211.** Smith at work shaping metal. **212.** Turning the millstone. **213.** Woman selling vegetables, flowers, etc. **214.** Shoemaker's workshop. **215.** The Roman theatre developed along more or less the same lines as it had in Greece. **216.** Roman in origin, the amphitheatre occupied an important place among the social distractions of the Romans: two gladiators in combat. **217.** A circus performance: a fight between two specially enraged lions. **218.** In the heart of Rome stood the Amphitheatrum Flavium, later called the Colosseum (see **186**) **219.** The arch at Benevento (see **173**) represents the main Roman deities: Jupiter, Juno, Minerva, Hercules, Bacchus, Ceres, and Mercury. **220.** A frequently observed religious ceremony was the Suevotaurilia, a purification rite in which a pig, a sheep, and a bull were sacrificed.

Neoplatonism. At the other extreme men's minds were attracted by various brands of superstition, especially astrology and a blind belife in fate and the stars. From such constricting and often terrifying beliefs some men found escape in religion. In a world in which countless deities and their cults flourished, some attempt at order was made through Syncretism by fusing cults together (thus in Britain a Roman and a Celtic deity might be identified: Mars and Cocidius). But the chief feature of the age was the spread of Oriental religions, those of Isis and Serapis from Egypt, Cybele from Asia, and Mithras from Persia. While these cults were claiming numerous adherents, another religion began to win the hearts and minds of men. After the death of its founder (ca. A.D. 30) Christianity was preached by the early missionaries in Asia, Syria, Greece, and Rome itself. The first persecution under Nero was followed by other intermittent and local attacks, but in the second century primitive Christianity began to develop into a well-organised 'catholic' church which spread its influence throughout the whole Empire.

THE LATER EMPIRE

With the murder of Commodus, who left no son or heir, Rome was faced with a situation not unlike that which resulted from the extinction of the Julio-Claudian dynasty at Nero's death. The Senate was powerless to prevent civil war when provincial armies put forward their commanders as rival candidates for the throne: Clodius Albinus in Britain, Pescennius Niger in Syria, and Septimius Severus, of African origin, in Pannonia. Before long Severus had gained Rome, defeated his rivals, and established a dynasty, the Severi. The importance of his reign (193–211) was that he gave up all pretence of working with the Senate and revealed to all that his authority derived merely from the support of the army: the civilian constitution that Augustus had worked out for the Empire was abandoned. In his task of strengthening the frontiers he restored order in northern Britain and died at York. His son Caracalla (211–17) by an edict in 212 abolished all distinction between Italian and provincials, so that all members of the Empire enjoyed Roman citizenship: his motive was less liberal than practical, to increase taxation. The attempt of Alexander Severus (221–35) to co-operate with the Senate failed to reverse the triumph of the military over the civil element, and his murder was followed by a few decades of military anarchy which threatened the very survival of the Roman Empire. The armies put forward their own candidates in bewildering numbers; they included a Thracian peasant Maximinus (235–38), the Arabian Philip (224–49), the Illyrian Decius (249–51), and the Moor Aemilianus (253). Meantime the Empire was assailed by barbarians from without and began to break up within. A new dynasty, the Sassanids, succeeded that of the Arsacids in Parthia, and moved to the attack: they overran Syria, captured the Roman Emperor Valerian who had advanced against them (259), and invaded Asia Minor. They were checked with help from the caravan city of Palmyra; but then its ruler, Zenobia, proceeded to challenge Roman authority in the East. In the West, Franks threatened the Lower Rhine, Saxons attacked shipping in the English Channel, Goths raided the Balkans and the Aegean. Alamanni crossed the Rhine and ravaged north Italy as far as Ravenna, and under the lead of a pretender named Postumus Gaul broke away from the Empire and with Spain and Britain formed an independent Gallic Empire. Only men of heroic resolution could have faced the problems of this crumbling world. Gallienus (253–68), despite a swarm of pretenders, managed to stop the rot, and under his Illyrian successors the tide turned. Claudius Gothicus repelled the Goths; Aurelian (270–75) had to evacuate Dacia, but by destroying Palmyra and recovering Gaul he earned his title of Restitutor Orbis. But the fact that Aurelian had to build a great wall around Rome itself, which had been free from foreign invasion since the days of Hannibal, showed only too clearly in what jeopardy the *pax Romana* stood. Although some dangers were surmounted, internal dissensions and barbarian pressure continued. Finally, out of a welter of short-lived Emperors Diocletian emerged and managed to hold power for twenty years (284–305) before voluntarily retiring. This achievement was won at the cost of radical reform. The Empire and the power of the Emperor were divided, and a system known as the tetrarchy was evolved. Diocletian became joint Augustus with Maximian, taking charge himself of the East and leaving the West to his colleague. In order to secure peaceful transference of power in the future, each Augustus took a junior Caesar who would in turn become an Augustus when his senior either died or retired. Although this plan provided a breathing space, in fact when Diocletian insisted on retiring, civil wars again broke out. In these Constantine finally, by his defeat of Maxentius at the battle of the Milvian Bridge, gained the Western Empire in 312, while supremacy was won in the East when Licinius defeated Maximinus in 313. But the two victors, although brothers-in-law, soon quarrelled. Licinius was defeated in 314 and then again finally in 324. The Empire was at last united under a resolute ruler. The centre of gravity, however, had been shifting from Italy to the East. Barbarian attacks had prevented Emperors from spending much time in Rome, and Diocletian had set up his court at Nicomedia in Bithynia. Constantine took the final logical step, and by 330 he had founded at Byzantium a new capital, East Rome or Constantinople.

The nature of the Emperor's power had profoundly changed: he was no longer Princeps but Dominus. In order to find an outward sanction for military usurpation, Emperors turned to Eastern ideas of a king as the viceregent of heavenly authority. Thus Aurelian had introduced into Rome the Persian cult of the Unconquered Sun, and Diocletian considered himself as Jovius, the earthly representative of Jupiter. With Constantine a further important step was taken. The long, intermittent but at times terrible persecution of the Christians by the Imperial government ended. The policy of repression had failed, and Constantine acknowledged the fact. To what extent he himself was converted to Christianity may be doubtful, but he believed that he owed his decisive victory in 312 to the God of the Christians, and henceforth he reigned as the earthly representative of that God. Thus a way was now open for a reconciliation between the Christian Church and the culture of the ancient world. The Emperor's authority, now legally autocratic, was also assuming a very different outward form from that of the Principate of Augustus. Aurelian, who was *dominus et deus*, introduced Oriental pomp, while Diocletian and Constantine developed an elaborate court ceremonial. The Emperor wore diadem, purple, and gold; his person became 'sacred'; and those admitted to audience had to prostrate themselves before their ruler. The old *consilium principis* became a *sacrum consistorium*. Vestiges of the Republic might survive in name. The Senate retained great prestige, but had scarcely more authority than a local town council, and any surviving Republican magistracies retained little executive authority. Military were separated from civilian offices, and under Constantine the senatorial and equestrian orders virtually merged. Great changes were also effected in the administration of the provinces, which were gradually increased, by division, to 116 and were governed by *praesides* or *rectores*. The provinces were grouped into twelve 'dioceses', each of which was under a *vicarius*, and the dioceses in turn were linked in four prefectures under four praetorian prefects. In the provinces impoverishment, financial pressure, and the spread of bureaucracy led to a decline in the municipal pride and self-government that had been such a fine feature of the earlier Empire. Under Constantine the unfortunate local senators (*curiales*) were made into a hereditary caste, and any attempt to avoid the crushing responsibility of office was forbidden. It is true that the Empire was guarded by an army against the worst attacks of the barbarians; but apart from the crucial fact that it was the army's reckless attempts to play the game of emperor making that had undermined the whole stability of the Empire itself, the nature and structure of the army had changed. It had long lost its national character. Differences between legions and *auxilia* had disappeared; under Gallienus senators had been removed from commands; the number of barbarian recruits increased; and finally it was divided into frontier forces (*limitanei*), who soon became mere local militias, and a mobile reserve field army (*comitatenses*). Under Constantine also the Praetorian Guard was disbanded.

The political collapse in the mid-third century was accompanied by an alarming economic collapse. Increased costs of administration led the central authorities to devalue the coinage and to develop a system of requisitioning and compulsory direction of labour. The whole monetary system was undermined, and in part was replaced by barter and payment in kind. However, thanks to the improvement of the coinage under Diocletian and Constantine, a money economy was gradually restored and confidence revived. As a remedy for the injustices that arbitrary requisitions had provoked, Diocletian introduced a new taxation system, the *annona* that was largely a levy in kind. This proved efficient but oppressive, especially as its collection became a compulsory corporate responsibility. This principle was gradually extended to other services, and various industrial and commercial guilds were made into hereditary corporations into which if need be men could be conscripted. The state also began to exercise similar direct control over agricultural workers. Taxes could not be collected if tenants, unable to fulfil their obligations to their landlords, fled and left the land untenanted. The government therefore intervened: tenants (*coloni*) on the large estates had to surrender their liberty of movement and sank to a state of serfdom (the colonate), bound to the land. The whole of society was falling into two classes: *honestiores* and *humiliores*. The former included Imperial and municipal senators, soldiers and veterans; they enjoyed many legal privileges. Each class in the state was carefully regulated in what was virtually a totalitarian system. In order to support the bureaucracy and the army, taxes

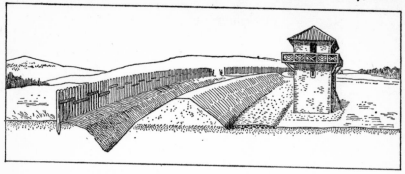

Reconstruction of a fortified frontier (*limes*) with watch-tower.

had to be levied, and in order to secure their payment and to exact the work necessary for the continuance of the state a large part of the population was bound in castes, as *collegiati, curiales,* or *coloni,* except for the lucky few who managed to escape into the privileged army, civil service, or church. Initiative withered; economic life declined; the total cultivated area, and the size of the towns, diminished. Naturally not all parts of the Empire declined as rapidly as did some, and there was another side to the picture. If social life declined in the towns, it flourished among the country aristocracy. Immense private estates had increased, and many senators continued to live in luxury in fortified villas on estates worked by *coloni.* The senatorial order enjoyed many immunities and considerable independence; these great landed proprietors became known as *potentiores,* the 'more powerful', and their life foreshadows medieval feudalism.

Cultural life naturally declined during the disturbed days of the third-century breakdown; but thereafter both Latin and Greek literature enjoyed a mild revival, and Christian literature showed great vigour. The fourth century produced such poets as Claudian and Ausonius, and the last great Roman historian, Ammianus Marcellinus of Antioch, who covered the period A.D. 96–378. Sculpture may have declined, but architecture maintained a high level of competence, and the way was prepared for 'late classical art'. The development of Roman law also had enduring results. Treatises on law were written by Papinian, Ulpian, and Paulus at the beginning of the third century, and these provided the material for the *Digest* which formed part of the great codification of

Roman law that was ordered by Justinian and carried out by Tribonian (530–4). This massive achievement had a profound influence on the later world when after the Dark Ages it was rediscovered at the end of the eleventh century and the knowledge widely applied from the fourteenth century in Continental Europe. The modern French and German codes are essentially, though not exclusively, based on Roman law. English law took an independent course; but even where direct inheritance is lacking, the two fundamental concepts of Roman law, reason and equity (*ratio* and *aequitas*), have played a major rôle in shaping Western culture. In the sphere of religious thought enduring changes were taking place. While paganism continued to flourish in country districts, Neoplatonism, Mithraism, and Christianity were striving to win men's minds or hearts. But when Constantine presided at the Council of Christian bishops at Nicaea in 325 it was clear which had gained the victory.

EPILOGUE

All divisions of history are more or less arbitrary, and there is no clear-cut demarcation line between ancient and medieval history. But many historians feel that when they come to the age of Diocletian and Constantine they are on the threshold of a world so different from the earlier classical world that a Roman Emperor presiding over a Christian Council in 325 symbolises in his person the beginning of a new era. Here we can take only a brief forward glance to the period when an increasing storm of blows gradually overthrew the Empire, which managed to survive for a century and a half in the West and for over a millennium in the East, where it saved Europe from the Turk.

Constantine's stupendous effort to maintain the restored unity of the Empire was doomed to failure. On his death in 337 war between his sons disrupted the Empire, which was again temporarily reunited under Constantius (in 351) and Julian, whose reign (361–4) saw a temporary reaction of paganism against Christianity. With Julian's death the Constantinian dynasty came to an end and the Empire again fell apart, the West under Valentinian (364–75) and the East under his brother Valens (364–78). It was once more united unter Theodosius I (395), whose sons, although in theory joint rulers of a single realm, were in practice monarchs of East and West. East and West gradually went their own ways. In the

East the Byzantine Empire survived until Constantinople was captured by the Mohammedans in 1453. The culture of the 'East Rome' became increasingly Greek, although it produced two of the greatest monuments of Roman law in the codes of Theodosius II and Justinian. Its obdurate resistance to barbarian attack not only secured it a thousand years of life, but enabled it to preserve and to hand on to the modern world so much of the legacy of the ancient world. The West, separated from the East and lacking the supplies of manpower that the East enjoyed in Asia Minor, could not long resist the mounting pressure of barbarian invasions. Britain, overrun by Picts, Scots, and Saxons, was abandoned by the Romans in 410. Gaul succumbed to Franks and Burgundians, Spain to Suebi and Vandals, who crossed over to North Africa in 429 and thus cut the Mediterranean world asunder. In 410 Alaric the Goth sacked Rome; in the eyes of Augustine the city 'made with hands' had fallen, while the city of God remained 'eternal in heaven'. Further disasters followed. Although Pope Leo in 452 managed to negotiate the withdrawal from Italy of Attila and his Huns, who had been weakened by a defeat in Gaul near Châlons the previous year, yet the Vandal Gaeseric raided and plundered Rome in 455. When the German Odoacer deposed the ruling Emperor Romulus Augustulus in 476, Rome's rule in the West ended. Even though this barbarian king ruled in Italy nominally in the name of the one Roman Emperor in Constantinople, and although in theory the latter might continue to regard the Empire as one and indivisible, in fact the division was complete. But it was only in Italy that Odoacer's power was recognised. The West had disintegrated, and Roman authority had disappeared from Britain, Gaul, Spain, Raetia, Noricum, and Africa. But so thoroughly had Gaul and Spain absorbed Roman culture that their use of the Latin language was not overwhelmed in the barbarian

221. The change in the distribution of power within the Empire is reflected in a diptych showing personifications of the old and new centres of power: Rome and Constantinople. 22. The Emperor Honorius, one of the first rulers of a separate Western half of the Empire, was threatened by Alaric and other invaders. 223. Ravenna, capital first of the Western Roman Emperors, then of Theodoric, king of the Ostrogoths, whose mausoleum has survived intact in Ravenna. 224. Justinian, who won back large parts of the old Empire, ruled from Byzantium; his reign is important because of his codification of Roman law. 225. Earlier building styles lived on in a new form: interior of Sant' Apollinare in Classe, built on old basilican lines. 226. New buildings were now sanctuaries of the victorious religion: Qalat Sem'an, a Christian place of pilgrimage in Syria. 227. Sarcophagus of 6th cent. with three monograms of Christ.

221

222

223

24

25

226

227

229

230

231

232

233

234

flood but survived to develop into the Romance languages. The Romanisation of the West was one of the most enduring monuments of the work of Augustus.

The downfall of the Roman Empire has stimulated the imagination of later ages and provoked constant speculation about its causes in general. In particular men have wondered why the West collapsed when it did, while the East managed to survive so much longer. Amid a welter of contributory factors no one basic cause can be isolated. Some have seen a decisive cause in climatic changes, soil exhaustion, disease, moral decline, race mixture, race suicide and lack of manpower, class warfare, educational errors, oppressive bureaucracy and the decline of municipal government, the undermining of a martial spirit by Oriental cults and Christianity, or even a determinist pattern of growth and decay which must affect all civilisations. But whether the causes be sought in the political, economic, social, religious, philosophic, or military fields, a most obvious symptom was the failure to maintain and control an adequate army. If the civilian authority could not guarantee an efficient military system, for whatever reasons, the barbarians must conquer.

But not all perished. The Latin language survived to provide an international channel of communication throughout the Middle Ages for men of learning and the clergy. Much Latin literature survived, however neglected it may have been at times. The Roman Catholic Church survived, with its organisation based partly upon that of the Roman Empire. Roman law survived to form the basis of most of the codes of Europe today. Throughout the Dark Ages the memory of imperial Rome remained a potent force, and it was largely through Rome that modern European culture, which derives so much from the Graeco-Roman world, gained its heritage.

How Roman civilisation left its imprint on large stretches of Europe, Africa, and western Asia can still be seen from the many remains that have been widely preserved. A Roman aqueduct still crosses Segovia in Spain (228). The aerial photograph (229) shows the theatre and amphitheatre at Arles in France. Trier in Germany was an important centre, even an Imperial residence for a time; the Porta Nigra there (230) testifies to Rome's power. 231. Amphitheatre at Caerleon in Wales. 232. Leptis Magna in Tripolis, a well-planned city where the theatre forms an imposing ruin. 233. A prominent lady of Palmyra, a main cultural and commercial centre in the East. 234. Pergamum, a leading city even in Hellenistic times, became the point of departure of Roman expansion in the East after Attalus III bequeathed his kingdom to the Romans. One of the ruins: a colonnade in the Aesculapium.

NOTES TO THE PLATES

The notes which follow refer only to those plates for which the revelant information could not be included in the actual captions. The following abbreviations are used: A.M. = Acropolis Museum; B.M. = British Museum; Cap. = Museo Capitolino; Gl. = Glyptothek; L. = Louvre; Lat. = Museo Laterano; M.M. = Metropolitan Museum; M.T. = Museo delle Terme; N.M. = National Museum; P.d.C. = Palazzo dei Conservatori; Vat. = Vatican Museum. The plates 112, 178, 189, 190, 197, 193 and 231 Copyright Dr. St. Joseph.

2. The bed of the Eurotas near Sparta in summer. **3.** Turkish bridge over the river Alpheus. **5.** The temple of Apollo at Bassae, probably by the same architect as the Parthenon (Ictinus); 425–400 B.C. **6.** Mountain ridges to the north of the Corinth Canal. **7.** The northern tip of the island of Amorgos in the Aegean Sea. **8.** The coast of Attica near Sunium. **9.** The Athenian Acropolis viewed from the stadium. **10.** The northern side of the Athenian Acropolis. **11.** The Acropolis viewed from the direction of the Hill of the Muses. **12.** Southern Italian landscape to the southeast of Paestum. **15–18.** Objects from the N.M., Heraklion. **27.** The Lion Gate at Mycenae, dating from ca. 1350 B.C. The gate (10¼ × 9¾ ft.) is formed by four monoliths. The lions, among the earliest Greek sculptures known, stand on either side of a column which tapers towards the base. Their forepaws rest on an altar and their heads are turned towards the visitor approaching the citadel. The heads, probably made of another material, were secured to the relief with pegs. **28.** Gold mask from Mycenae, about 11¾ in. high. N.M., Athens. **29.** Mycenaean soldiers portrayed on a vase. **32.** Rhapsode during a performance. Fragment of an Attic red-figure amphora found at Vulci; 480 B.C. B.M., London. **33.** Women kneading dough, Boeotian terracotta of late 7th cent. B.C. L., Paris. **34.** Boeotian terracotta horse; ca. 600 B.C. Private collection. **35.** Bronze equestrian statuette, rider and horse cast separately; horse's legs restored. Southern Italian work in Greek style; 550 B.C. B. M., London. **36.** Woman athlete, probably winner of a race; third quarter of 6th cent. B.C., from northwest Greece; left leg restored. B.M., London. **37.** Fragment of a geometric vase, showing a mourning scene; 8th cent. B.C. N.M., Athens. **38.** Greek black-figure amphora by Amasis; ca. 540 B.C. Bibliothèque Nationale, Paris. **39.** Greek black-figure amphora by Amasis; ca. 540 B.C. Achilles slaying Penthesilea. B.M., London. **40.** Kouros, found in Attica; 615–600 B.C. M.M., New York. **41.** Kore in long chiton and peplos, found on the Acropolis; late 6th cent. B.C.; it still has traces of the original colouring. A.M., Athens. **42.** Head of a kore; ca. 530 B.C. A.M., Athens. **43.** Head of the 'Apollo of Tenea', found in ancient Tenea, near Corinth; mid 6th cent. B.C. Gl., Munich. **44–45.** Head of Zeus, from Olympia; 6th cent. B.C. N.M. Athens. **47.** Doric temple of Poseidon at Paestum (southern Italy); 6th cent. B.C. **48.** Temple of Aphaea on the island of Aegina; ca. 500 B.C. First excavated in 1811. Most of the statues from the temple are now in the Gl., Munich. **49.** Dying warrior from the west façade of the temple of Aphaea on Aegina; ca. 500 B.C. Gl., Munich. **50.** The battlefield of Marathon. 1. The Cynosura (= dog's tail), a narrow spit of land behind which the Persians anchored their fleet for protection against wind and current. From here they moved into the marshy plain. When news of the landing reached them, the Athenians occupied the hills on the southeastern side (2), whence they marched against the Persians who had formed up in the middle of the plain (3). **51.** The Pass of Thermopylae, now much wider than in classical times as a result of alluvial deposit (the ground in the bottom right-hand corner of the photograph). **52.** Vertical aerial photograph of the Strait of Salamis (from the *American Journal of Archaeology*). **53.** A helmeted hoplite, fragment from the north frieze of the Treasury of Siphnos at Delphi. Parian marble, found in 1894. Museum, Delphi. **54.** Fragment of a vase by Sophilos, with scenes from the funeral games for Patroclus; ca. 570 B.C. N.M., Athens. **55.** Top part of the krater of Vix, found in 1952 in a Celtic burial mound at Vix (Côte-d'Or). This hugh voluted krater is almost 6 ft. high; 6th cent. B.C. Museum, Châtillon-sur-Seine. **56.** View of the Athenian Acropolis with important buildings of classical and Roman times reconstructed to show the appearance as it once was. **57.** The same view as it now is. **59.** Owl of Athena on a tetradrachm; 6th cent. B.C. **60.** Fragment of Selene's quadriga, from the east façade of the Parthenon; ca. 432 B.C. B.M., London. **61.** Fragment from the north frieze of the Parthenon. B.M., London. **62.** Fragment of a votive relief from Melos; ca. 465 B.C. N.M., Athens. **63.** The 'Fairhaired Epebe', N.M., Athens. **64.** The Erechtheum with the Porch of the Caryatids on the Athenian Acropolis; 425–400 B.C. **65.** The temple of Nike on the Athenian Acropolis, 415 B.C. **66.** Figure of Athena by Myron. Städelscher Kunstinstitut, Frankfort-on-Main. **69.** Top edge of a red-figure Attic krater with representation of Hector's death, found at Cerveteri; ca. 490 B.C. B.M., London. **70.** Grave lekythos showing a girl, called 'the beautiful' in the inscription, looking at a fillet. B.M., London. **71.** A bowl by Hieron and Makron, late 5th cent. B.C. Staatliche Museen, Berlin. **73.** An Athenian prize amphora with four runners; 6th cent. B.C. Berlin. **74.** Reconstruction of the sanctuary at Olympia, showing the temple of Zeus, other shrines, treasuries, etc. **75.** Reconstruction of the sanctuary of Apollo at Delphi, superimposed on a photograph of the site in its present condition. **76.** View from the stadium at Delphi; the valley of the Plistos and the Gulf of Itea can be seen in the background. **77.** General view of the sanctuary of Apollo on the island of Delos. In the foreground the walled sacred lake, and, behind it, the Agora of the Italians; to the right of the latter, the Lion Terrace with a number of the original lion statues. In the background houses and other buildings of the city of Delos. **78.** The 'relief of the Delian deities'. Many parts have been restored. Apollo, followed by Artemis and Leto (one with a torch, the other with a sceptre) holds out a bowl to Nike into which she pours a libation. Beside Nike an altar or base with a relief of the Horae or Charites. On the left the illustration is bounded by a column on which stands a tripod. The column is joined by a wall surrounding a temple domain. Above this wall projects part of a temple with Corinthian columns and a frieze depicting chariot racing. This is probably a representation of the sanctuary on Delos. Opinion about the dating is divided; the relief is probably part of an earlier (5th cent. B.C.) work, while the background and Nike were added in Roman times. **79.** Relief dedicated in honour of Asclepius by a man cured of a foot disease. According to another theory it represents a shoemaker. B.M., London. **80.** The theatre at Epidaurus, built in the 4th cent. B.C. by Polyclitus. **83.** Actor dressed as a woman; marble relief; 350–325 B.C. Ny Carlsberg Gl., Copenhagen. **84.** Fragment of a vase showing a theatre scene; 400–375 B.C., Museum, Bologna. **85.** Music lesson, fragment of a hydria, painted by Phintias; ca. 510 B.C. **86.** Side of a black-figure bowl, showing a pirate ship overtaking a merchant vessel; ca. 540 B.C. B.M., London. **89.** The peninsula of Ortygia. This was the main centre of Syracuse when, in its heyday, it stretched far inland. **90.** Sparta, protected by the Taygetus Mts. **91.** Corinth as seen from the Acrocorinth. **97.** Doryphoros (man carrying a spear) by Polycleitus; a copy. N.M., Naples. **98.** Diadumenos (man putting a fillet round his head) by Polycleitus. N.M., Athens. **99.** Fragment of a relief by Praxiteles, from Mantinea; last quarter of 4th cent. B.C. N.M., Athens. **100.** The rape of the daughters of Leucippus, fragment of a bowl by Medias, first quarter of 4th cent. B.C. B.M., London. **101.** Heracles by Scopas, from Tegea; ca. 375 B.C. Museum, Tegea. **107.** Boxer's head, attributed to Silanion, found at Olympia; 2nd half of 4th cent. B.C. N.M., Athens. **103.** Tombstone of Hegeso, found in the Dipylon cemetery at Athens; ca. 400 B.C. N.M., Athens. **104.** Lion of Chaeronea, erected in classical times. Dug up at the end of last century, restored and re-erected on the same site. **105.** Alexander the Great. Museo Baracco, Rome. **106.** Temple of Apollo at Didyma in Asia Minor. **112.** Scenes from the life of Buddha, the 'Gandhara relief', so called after the district of that name in India; 2nd cent. A.D. Institute of Arts, Detroit. **113.** Aerial photograph of Alexandria. The white lines indicate the street plan of the ancient city. **115.** The 'Feeding of Telephus', one of the most important wall-paintings found in the basilica of Herculaneum. Left: allegorical figure of Arcadia; behind her a satyr with a syrinx. Telephus is being suckled by a hind. Right: Heracles, behind him Nemesis or Parthenos. N.M., Naples. **116.** Fight between Amazons and Giants, on an altar at Pergamum; erected ca. 180 B.C. by Eumenes II. Berlin. **117.** The 'jockey of Artemisium'; 2nd cent. B.C. N.M., Athens. **118.** Dying Gaul. Cap., Rome. **119.** Relief of a triumphal procession. Groups of horsemen and lictors with the goddess Roma. Flavian period. Vat., Rome. **120.** Soldier, from a bronze pot; Etruscan work; 6th cent. B.C., from Perugia. Gl., Munich. **121.** Figure of a lion, detail of an Etruscan gold fibula. **126.** Sarcophagus with husband and wife; 6th–5th cent. B.C. Museo Villa Giulia, Rome. **127.** Flute-player from the 'Tomb of the Leopards'; 1st half of 5th cent. B.C. Tarquinia. **128.** The 'Capitoline wolf'; late 6th century B.C., Etruscan. The figures representing Romulus and Remus were added in Renaissance times. **129.** Altar from Ostia, showing Romulus and Remus being suckled by the wolf. Alongside lies the god Tiber, with his left hand resting on a water-jug. Two shepherds look on. Above the shepherds is a symbolic representation of the Palatine hill, with a local deity and the Roman eagle; ca. A.D. 125 M.T., Rome **130.** Relief showing the birth of Romulus and Remus, with Rhea Silvia lying beside the Tiber. Mars, surrounded by cupids and torchbearers, alights beside her: early 3rd cent. A.D. Vat. **132.** Urn in the form of a house. Museo Villa Giulia, Rome. **134.** Farmer ploughing. Etruscan work, 6th cent. B.C. Peasants still use similar ploughs. Museo Villa Giulia, Rome. **135.** Two soldiers from Rome's earliest history, with fallen comrade. Etruscan handle from a bronze chest; 4th cent. B.C. L., Paris. **136.** Etruscan head of a Maenad, archaic antefix from Aracoeli on the Capitol at Rome. P.d.C., Rome. **137.** Bearded deity from the temple of Mater Matuta at Satricum, 5th cent. B.C. Museo Villa Giulia, Rome. **141–142.** Silver coins with African elephants, struck by the Carthaginians at Carthago Nova in Spain; 221–218 B.C. B.M., London. **143.** View of Saguntum looking in an easterly direction along the walls. The walls built at a later date undoubtedly follow the line of those that existed in Hannibal's time. The Roman and the modern towns lie between the hill and the river. **144.** Hieron of Syracuse, silver coin. Staatl. Münzkabinett, Munich. **145.** View of Cannae and environs with the plain of the Aufidus. **146.** Relief depicting the battle of Pydna. Museum, Delphi. **147.** Campanian bowl with Indian war elephant. Museo Villa Giulia, Rome. **150.** Gallo-Roman soldier. L., Paris. **156.** Pompeius Magnus. Ny Carlsberg Gl., Copenhagen. **157.** Gaius Julius Caesar, probably an Egyptian work. Museo Baracco, Rome. **158.** Sepulchral stele with seven members of a Roman family. Museum, Ravenna. **159.** Bust of a man; Republican period. L., Paris. **160.** The 'Maison Carrée', built at Nîmes in 16 B.C. **161.** The Forum Boarium at Rome with (*left*) a temple originally dedicated to Vesta and later converted into a church, (*centre*, in background) remains of the 'house of Crescentius', and (*right*) the temple of Fortuna Virilis. **162.** Fresco with architectural motifs to give an illusion of increased spaciousness; from Pompeii. N.M., Naples. **163.** Stucco work in the vault of the vestibulum of the subterranean basilica near the Porta Maggiore at Rome; ca. A.D. 20. **164.** Cameo known as the 'Gemma Augustea', showing Augustus enthroned beside the goddess Roma, with various figures beside and behind him. Also behind him is the sign of Capricorn, under which he was born. On the extreme left a chariot with the goddess Victoria and Tiberius. Germanicus stands beside Roma. On the lower part Roman soldiers are seen erecting a symbol of victory, while bearded prisoners of war look on. Museum, Vienna. **165.** Fragment of the frieze of the Ara Pacis at Rome, showing a number of priests and members of the Imperial family, including Agrippa, Julia, Tiberius and Lucius Caesar; 9 B.C. **166.** Marble panel found under the Palazzo della Cancellaria; 2nd cent. A.D. Tabularium, Rome. **167.** Roman aqueduct (Pont du Gard) near Nîmes in southern France. The bridge, built in three tiers of arches, carries a water course over the river Gardon. Probably built by Agrippa. **168.** Triumphal arch erected at Susa, northern Italy, in honour of Augustus. **169.** Mosaic showing (*top*) a cat killing a partridge and (*bottom*) two ducks, from Pompeii. N.M., Naples. **170.** Fragment of one of the many mosaics found in a villa – probably an Emperor's – at Piazza Armerina on Sicily; ca. A.D. 300. **171.** Fragment of a sarcophagus found at Acilia, between Rome and Ostia, in 1950. Opinions differ as to what it represents. It is a Philosophers or marriage sarcophagus which was probably kept in store, ready made except for the portraits, which could be applied later. This would account for the fact that the front figure, probably the Emperor Gordianus II, has the head of a boy but the body of an adult. Another theory is that the sarcophagus belonged to a certain Carinus, that he and his wife are portrayed and that the figure at the corner is his son Nigzinianus(?). Dated to the last quarter of the 3rd cent. A.D. M.T., Rome. **174.** Vault of the Arch of Trajan at Benevento. **176.** Fort, now called Qasr al-Her, near Palmyra in Syria. The walls and towers are partly preserved; 2nd cent. A.D. **177.** The 'Portico Circolare' in the villa built by Hadrian at Tibur (Tivoli). **178.** Hadrian's Wall at Housesteads, Northumberland. **180.** Equestrian games (*decursiones*) on the base of a column erected in memory of Antoninus Pius. **183.** Diocletian. Cap., Rome. **184.** Head of a colossal statue of Constantine the Great. P.d.C., Rome. **185.** Fragment of a relief on the sepulchral monument of the Aterii, probably representing temples lining the Via Sacra; late 1st cent. A.D. Lat., Rome. **199.** Relief bearing a travel scene. Musée Calvet, Avignon. **200–201.** Mosaics on the Piazzale delle Corporazioni at Ostia; 2nd cent. A.D. **202.** 'House of the Masks' on Delos; ca. A.D. 100. **203.** Fresco from the 'House of Livia' showing a garden with fruit trees and birds. Reconstruction by Gismondo of tenements at Ostia. **204–205** Ruins of houses and tenements at Ostia. **207.** Mosaic from 'the House of the Masks', showing Dionysus riding on a panther. The mosaic artist has captured with extraordinary success the lithe and ferocious quality of the beast and the elaborate folds of the god's clothing. Dionysus carries the thyrsus (a pine cone on a wand) and a cymbal, both traditionally associated with his cult. **208.** Floral still-life from Pompeii. Mosaic. N.M., Naples. **209.** Marriage ceremony, fragment of sarcophagus. Campo Santo, Pisa. **210.** Husband and wife at a meal. Stele of C. Julius Maternus. Museum, Cologne. **211.** Smithy. On the left an assistant blows up the fire with a bellows; on the right, tools used by the smith and a lock. Vat., Rome. **212.** Fragment of a sarcophagus showing a grindstone being turned. Vat., Rome. **213.** Woman vendor. Lapidarium, Ostia. **214.** Shoemaker's workshop. M.T., Rome. **215.** Relief showing tragic and comic masks for use on stage. Vat., Rome. **216.** Two gladiators. Each wears a helmet with a visor, a cloak folded in three, a belt, and leg-guards. Probably from Ephesus. **217.** Terracotta relief showing *Bestiarii* fighting with a lion and lioness in a circus. Seven 'eggs' stand on two pillars; one egg was removed after each round. M.T., Rome. **218.** Reconstruction of the Amphitheatum Flavium. Fragment of the reconstruction of Rome. Museo della Civiltà Romana, Rome. **219.** Fragment of Trajan's Arch at Benevento: Jupiter (with sceptre and thunderbolt), Juno (with veil), Minerva (with helmet), Hercules (with club), Bacchus (with crown of grapes), Ceres (with wreath of ears of corn), and Mercury (with rod). **220.** Suevotaurilia. Rome, Forum; 3rd cent. A.D. **221.** Personifications of the cities of Rome and Constantinople; ivory diptych; ca. A.D. 469. Kunsthistorisches Museum, Vienna. **222.** The Emperor Honorius, part of diptych of Probus. Cathedral, Aosta. **224.** Fragment of mosaic in the San Vitale at Ravenna, A.D. 530. **227.** Christian sarcophagus with Christian ornaments. Apollinare in Classe, Ravenna. **233.** Upper-class woman of Palmyra; 2nd cent. A.D. Ny Carlsberg Gl., Copenhagen.

INDEX

Figures in italics refer to the Plates. Names in italics in brackets are classical forms.

A

Abydos, Map 5, 6
Academy, 99
Acarnania, 68 (Fig.); Maps 2, 6
Achaean League, 102
Achaeans, 14
Achaia, 68 (Fig.); Maps 1, 2, 4, 6, 12, 13
Achelous, Maps 1, 2
Achilles, 25
Acragas (*Lat.* Agrigentum), 68; Map 9
Acritas Pr., Map 1
Acrite, Map 1
Acropolis (Athens), 66, 71; *9, 10, 11, 56–8*
Acte, Map 1
Actium, 164; Map 12
Adramyttium, Maps 1, 6
Adria, Maps 9, 14
Adriatic Sea (*Mare Adriaticum*), 132, Maps 9, 14
Aegae, 68 (Fig.); Map 1
Aegean Sea (*Mare Aegaeum*), 10, 11–13, 26–8, 84, 211; Map 1
Aegates I., 132; Map 14
Aegina, 66; Maps 1, 2, 6
Aegosthena, *94*; Map 1
Aemilia, Map 14
Aemilianus, 211
Aeneid, 178
Aenus, Mt., Map 1
Aeolians, 26; Map 2
Aequi, 119, 120; Map 9
Aeschines, 88, 99
Aeschylus, 82
Aetna, Mt., Map 14
Aetolia, Maps 1, 2, 4, 6
Aetolian League, 102
Africa, 130–1, 163, 216; (Rom. province), 135, 151, 180; Maps 12, 13
Agamemnon, 25
Agathe, Map 14
ager publicus, 149
Agesilaus, 85

Agora (Athens), *67–8*
Agricola, 193
Agri Decumates, 193; Map 13
Agrigentum, 68; Map 9, 10, 14
Agrippa, 179, 181
Agrippina, 182, 183
Alalia, 114
Alaric, 216
Alba Fucens, *138–9*
Albania, Map 13
Alcaeus, 43
Alcibiades, 84
Alcman, 43
Alemanni, 211
Aleria, Map 14
Alesia, Map 11
Alexander (king of Macedon), 97–8; *105, 108*
Alexandria, 97, 101, 103, 163; *113*; Maps 7, 8, 11, 13
Alexandria, Library of, 101, 103
Alexandria Eschate, Map 7
Allia, 120
Alpes, Maps 12, 13, 14
Alpheus, *4*; Map 1
Alps, 12, 133
Ambracia, Maps 1, 6
Ambracius, Sinus, Map 1
Ammianus Marcellinus, 214
Ammonium, Map 7
Amorgos, Map 1
Amphipolis, 70, 84, 88; Map 1
Amphyctionic Leagues, 27, 88
Anaxagoras, 82
Anaximenes, 54
Ancona, Map 14
Ancyra, Map 13
Andros, 68 (Fig.), 70; Maps 1, 2, 6
Anio, Map 14
Antigonids, 101
Antigonus Gonatas, 101
Antioch (*Antiochia*), 101; Maps 8, 13

Antiochus I (king of Syria), 101
Antiochus III (king of Syria), 134
Antipolis, Map 14
Antium, Map 14
Antonine Wall, 195
Antoninus Pius, 195
Antony, Mark, 164–5; *152*
Aornos, Map 7
'Apennine culture', 113
Apennines, 113, 114; Map 14
Aphaea, Temple of (Aegina), 30 (Fig.); *48–9*
Aphrodite of Melos, 103
Apollonia, Maps 6, 10, 12
Apollonius Rhodius, 103
Appia, Via, *182*
Appian, 209
Apuleius, 209
Apulia, Map 14
Aquae Sextiae, 151
Aquileia, 135; Maps 13, 14
Aquincum, Map 13
Aquitani, Map 11
Aquitania (Gaul), 180; Maps 12, 13
Arabia, 55 (Fig.); Maps 7, 8
Arabia Deserta, Map 13
Arabia Petraea, 194
Arabicus, Sinus, Map 13
Arachosia, 55 (Fig.); Maps 7, 8
Ara Pacis, 178, 179 (Fig.), 197 (Fig.); *165*
Arausio, 151
Arbela, 55 (Fig.)
Arcadia, 29, 85, 96; *4*; Maps 1, 2, 6
Arcadians, Map 2
Archilochus, 43
Archimedes, 103
architecture, Greek, 44; *46–9, 64–5*
architecture, Roman, 147–148, 167, 214; *167–8, 172–8, 202–8*
archons, 31

Arctonnesos, Map 1
Areion, Map 7
Arelate, Map 14
Areopagus, Court of the, 32, 33, 70
Argentarius, Mt., Map 14
Argolicus, Sinus, Map 1
Argolis, 68 (Fig.); Maps 1, 6
Argos, 28, 29, 69, 84; *93*; Maps 1, 2, 4, 6
Ariminum, Maps 9, 10, 14
Ariovistus, 163
Aristeides, 67
Aristophanes, 86–7
Aristotle, 99–100
Arles, theatre and amphitheatre at, *229*
Armenia, 55 (Fig.), 162, 183, 194; Maps 7, 8, 13
Arnus, Maps 10, 14
Arretium, Map 14
Arsacids, 211
art, Roman, 147–8, 166–7, 214; *158–66*
Artaxata, Map 13
Artemis, Temple of (Ephesus), 100
Artemisium, Maps 1, 5
Asculum, Map 9
Asia (Rom. province), 135, 136, 152; Maps 12, 13
Asia Minor, 13, 53, 54, 55, 67, 162, 211, 216
Asine, Map 1
Asopus, Map 1
Assus, Map 1
Assyria, 54, 194, 195; Map 13
astu, 11
Astypalaea, Map 1
Atax, Map 14
Aternum, Map 14
Atesis, Map 14
Athena, 25
Athena of Myron, *66*
'Athena Promachos', 71
Athens (*Athenae*), 13, 15, 26–8, 31–2, 41–2, 56, 65–72, 68 (Fig.), 81–7, 100, 101; *56–8*; Maps 1, 2, 4, 5, 6, 13
Athos, Mt., 65; Maps 1, 4
Atlanticus, Oceanus, Map 13
'Atreus, Treasury of', 15
Attalids, 101

Attalus III (king of Pergamum), 135
Attica, 32, 68 (Fig.), 83, 84; Maps 1, 2, 6
Aufidus, 133 (Fig.); Maps 10, 14
Augusta Treverorum, Map 13
Augusta Vindelicorum, Map 13
Augustonemetum, Map 14
Augustus, Octavianus, 168, 177–81
Aurelian, 211
Aurelius, Marcus, 195–6, 209; *179*
Axius, Map 1

B

Babylon, 55 (Fig.), 97, 98; Maps 7, 8, 13
Babylonia, 54, 55 (Fig.), 101; Map 8
Bactra, 55 (Fig.); Maps 7, 8
Bactria, 55 (Fig.); Maps 7, 8
Baecula, Map 10
Baetica (Spain), 180; Maps 12, 13
Baleares I., Maps 10, 14
Bassae, 5; Map 1
Batavi, Map 13
Belgae, Map 11
Belgica (Gaul), 180; Maps 12, 13
Benacus, Lacus, Map 14
Beneventum, Map 14
Bibracte, Map 11
Bithynia, 161; Maps 8, 12, 13
Boadicea, see BOUDICCA
Boeae, Map 1
Boeotia, 15, 27, 66, 68 (Fig.), 69–70, 84, 85, 86; Maps 1, 2, 6
Boii, 132
Bononia, 135; Maps 13, 14
Bospori, Regnum, Map 13
Bosporus, Cimmerian, 70
Bostra, Map 13
Boudicca, 183
Boulē (Council), 41, 42, 71, 81
Brigantes, 193
Britain (*Britannia*), 182, 183–4, 193, 195, 210, 211, 216; Maps 11, 12, 13
Britannicus, 182, 183

Britannicus, Oceanus, Map 13
Brundisium, Maps 11, 13, 14
Brutii, Map 14
Brutus, Marcus, 164; *154*
Bucephala, Map 7
Burdigala, Map 13
Burgundians, 216; Map 13
Byzantium (*Lat.* Constantinopolis), 88; Maps 1, 3, 6, 13

C

Caenepolis, Map 1
Caere, *122–4*; Map 9
Caerleon, amphitheatre at, *231*
Caesar, Gaius Julius, 162–4, 167; *157*
Caesaraugusta, Map 13
Caesarea (Caesariensis), Map 13
Caesarea (Judaea), Map 13
Caesariensis, Map 13
Calabria, Map 13
Calauria, Map 1
Caledonia, 193; Map 13
Caligula, 182
Callias, Peace of, 68
Callimachus, 103
Calymna, Map 1
Cambyses, 54
Camirus, Map 2
Campania, 114, 115, 116; Map 14
Camulodunum, 182
Cane, Mt., Map 1
Cannae, 133; *148*; Map 10
Cantabrians, 180
Carpathium, Mare, Map 1
Carpathos, Map 1
Capitoline hill, 116, 120, 197 (Fig.); *133, 172, 187*
'Capitoline Wolf', *128*
Cappadocia, 55 (Fig.), 182; Maps 8, 13
Capreae, Map 14
Capua, 133; Maps 9, 10, 13, 14
Caracalla, 210; *181*
Carales, Map 14
Caria, 55 (Fig.), 68 (Fig.), 88; Maps 1, 2, 4, 5, 6
Carrhae, 163
Carthage (*Carthago*), 9–10, 69, 98, 114, 130–4, 135; Maps 10, 11, 13

Carthage, New, see CAR-
THAGO NOVA
Carthago Nova, 134; Maps
10, 11, 13
Carystus, 69; Map 4
Casos, Map 1
Caspian Gates, 79; Map 7
Caspian Sea (*Mare Caspium*),
55 (Fig.), 103; Map 7
Cassius, 164
Catana, Map 14
Catiline, 162
Cato the Censor, 135, 147
Catullus, 167
Caucasus, Map 13
Caudine Forks, 120
Celsus, 209
Celtae, Map 11
Celtiberians, 135
Celts (Gallic tribes), 115,
120, 132
Cenchreae, Map 1
Ceos, Map 1
Cephallenia, 68 (Fig.);
Maps 1, 2, 6
Ceria, Map 1
Cerveteri, see CAERE
Chaeronea, 88; *104*
Chalcedon, Maps 1, 3, 6
Chalcidice, 27, 68 (Fig.),
86; Map 1
Chalcis, 28; Maps 1, 6
Chalôns, 216
Chaonia, Map 1
Chatti, Map 13
Chauci, Map 13
Chelonatas Pr., Map 1
Chersonese, Thracian, 70
Cherusci, Map 13
Chios, 26; Maps 1, 2, 4, 5
Christianity, 183, 196, 210,
212, 215, 225
Cicero, 162, 164, 167
Cilicia, 55 (Fig.), 161;
Maps 12, 13
Cimbri, 151
Cimolos, Map 1
Cimon, 67, 68
Circei, Map 14
Cirta, Maps 10, 13
Cispadana, Map 14
Cithaeron, Mt., Map 1
Civil Law, Roman, 149
Claudius I, 182
Claudius II, 211
Clazomenae, Maps 1, 2
Cleisthenes, 42

Cleomenes III (king of
Sparta), 102
Cleon, 84
Cleonae, Map 1
Cleopatra, 163, 164–5
cleruchies, 70
Clodius, 163
Clodius Albinus, 210
Clusium, 114; Map 9
Cnidus, 85; Maps 2, 6
Cnossus, 13–14; *13–22*;
Maps 1, 2
Colchis, Map 13
collegiati, 214
coloni, 213–14
colonisation, Greek, 26–7;
Maps 2, 3, 9
Colophon, Maps 1, 2, 6
Colosseum, 183 (Fig.), 193,
197 (Fig.); *186, 218*
Columela, 209
Comitia centuriata, 117
Constantine I, 211–12, 215;
184
Constantine, Arch of, *184*
Constantinople (*Constantino-
polis*), 212, 216
Constantius, 215
Commodus, 196
Comum, Map 14
Concilium Plebis, 117
Copais, Lacus, Map 1
Corassiae I, Map 1
Corcyra, 28, 83, 84, 86
(Fig.); Maps 1, 6
Corcyra Nigra, Map 9
Corduba, Map 13
Corfinium, Map 9
Corinth (*Corinthus*), 26, 28,
31, 66, 68 (Fig.), 69,
83, 102; *91*; Maps 1, 2,
6, 13
Corinthiacus, Sinus, Map 1
Corone, Map 1
Corsica, 56, 114, 135; Maps
10, 12, 13, 14
Cortona, Map 9
Cos, Maps 1, 2
Crassus, 152, 161–3
Cremona, Map 14
Crete, (*Creta*) 13–14, 25,
161; Maps 1, 2, 4, 5, 6,
13
Creticum, Mare, Map 1
Croesus, 54, 55
Croton, Maps 3, 9, 10, 14
Ctesiphon, Map 13

Cumae, 69, 114, 115; Maps
3, 9, 14
Cunaxa, 85
Curiales, 213, 214
Cyclades, Map 1
Cydonia, Maps 1, 6
Cylon, 32
Cyme, Maps, 1, 2, 6
Cynics, 100
Cynoscephalae, 134
Cyphanta, Map 1
Cyprus, 13, 26; Maps 8, 12,
13
Cyrenaica, Maps 12, 13
Cyrene, 27; *87*; Maps 3, 13
Cyrus (king of Persia), 54,
55
Cyrus the Younger, 85
Cythera, 68 (Fig.); Maps 1,
2, 6
Cythnos, Map 1
Cyzicus, Map 6

D

Dacia, 194, 195, 211; Map
13
Dacians, 164, 193, 194
Dalmatia, Map 13
Dalmatians, 135, 180
Damascus, 55 (Fig.), Maps
8, 13
Danube (*Danuvius*) (Danube
frontier), 180, 181, 193,
194, 195, 196; Maps 12,
13
Darius I (king of Persia),
54–6, 65
Darius II (king of Persia),
97
Decebalus, 194
Decelea, Map 1
Decius, 211
Delos, 67, 68 (Fig.), 70; 77–
78; Map 1
Delos, Confederacy of, 69–
70
Delphi, 28, 43; *75–6, 82*;
Maps 1, 2, 5, 6
Demeter, 53
Democritus, 82, 104
Demosthenes, 88, 99
Deva, Map 13
Diadochi kingdoms, 101–4
'Diadumenos' of Polycleitus,
98
Didyma, Map 2

Digest of Tribonian, 214–15
Dio Cassius, 209
Dio Chrysostom, 209
Diocletian, 211; *183*
Diogenes, 100
Dion, 98
Dionysian Festivals, 53
Dionysius I (king of Syracuse), 98
Dionysus, 53
Dionysus, Theatre of (Athens), 71 (Fig.); *81*
Dodona, Maps 1, 2, 6
Dolopes, Map 1
Dominate, 210–15
Domitian, 193–4
Dorians, 25–6, 87; Map 2
Doris, Map 1
'Doryphoros' of Polycleitus, 97
Draco, 32
drama, Greek, 82, 86–7, 99, 103
Drepana, 132; Map 14
Druidism, 196
Drusus, Marcus Livius, 151–2
Drusus Caesar, 181
Drusus Nero, Claudius, 180, 181
Dura-Europos, Map 13
'Dying Gaul' (Pergamum), *118*
Dyrrhachium, 163; Map 11

E

Eastern Roman Empire, 215–16
Eburacum, Map 13
Ebusus, Map 10
Ecbatana, Maps 7, 8
Ecclesia (Assembly), 32, 42, 81
Ecnomus Pr., Map 14
Egypt (*Aegyptus*), 9, 13, 25, 55 (Fig.), 67–8, 97, 100, 101, 102, 163, 164, 180; Maps 7, 8, 11, 12, 13
Elea, Map 9; see VELIA
Elis, Maps 1, 2
Elbe (*Albis*), 180; Maps 12, 13
Elymes, Map 9
Eleusis, Map 1
Emerita Augusta, Map 13

Empedocles, 82
Emporiae, Maps, 3, 10, 14
Ennius, 146–7
Epaminondas, 85
Ephesus, Maps 1, 2, 6, 13
ephors, 29
Epictetus, 209
Epicureanism, 148, 167, 209
Epicurus, 104
Epidamnus, Map 3
Epidaurus, *79*; Maps 1, 6
Epidaurus, Theatre of, 99 (Fig.); *80*
Epidaurus, Limera Map 1
Epirus, 129; Maps 1, 2, 4, 5, 6, 8
Equites, 135
Eratosthenes, 104
Erechtheum, 71 (Fig.); *64*
Eretria, 28, 56, 65; Maps 1, 4, 6
Erymanthus, Mt., Map 1
Erythrae, Maps 1, 6
Eryx, Map 14
Etruria, 114; Map 14
Etruscans, 69, 113–14, 116, 120; Map 9
Euboea, 28, 66, 68 (Fig.), 69, 70; Maps 1, 2, 4, 5, 6
Euclid, 103
Euphrates, Maps 8, 13
Euripides, 86
Eurotas, Map 1
Eurymedon, 67
Euxine (*Pontus Euxinus*), 26, 27, 55 (Fig.), 70; Maps 7, 13

F

Fabius Pictor, 147
Faesulae, Map 14
Fanum Fortunae, Map 14
'Feeding of Telephus' (Herculaneum), *115*
Felsina, Map 9
Firmum, Map 14
Flamininus, 146
Forum Boarium, *161*
Forum Iulii, Map 14
Forum Romanum, 115, 197 (Fig.); *187*
Fosse Way (Britain), *189*
Franks, 211
Frisii, Map 13
Fronto, 209

G

Gabinius, 162
Gades, Maps 10, 11, 13
Gaeseric, 216
Gaetulia, Maps 12, 13
Galatia, 180, 184; Maps 8, 12, 13
Galba, 184
Galen, 209
Gallicus, Sinus, Map 14
Gallienus, 211, 213
Gandhara sculptures, *112*
Garamantes, Map 13
Gargarus, Mt., Map 14
Garumna, Map 10
Gaugamela, 97; Map 7
Gaul (*Gallia*), 162–3, 180, 211, 216; Maps 10, 13, 14
Gaul, Cisalpine, 12, 115, 135, 166
Gaul, Transalpine, 163
Gauls, 135
Gedrosia, 55 (Fig.), 98; Maps 7, 8
Gela, Maps 9, 14
Gelon, 68, 69
'Gemma Augustea', *164*
Genua, Maps 13, 14
Georgics, 178
Geranea, Mt., Map 1
Germania, Maps 11, 12, 13
Germanicus, Oceanus, Map 13
Germans, 151, 181, 196; Map 11
Germany, Lower, 194; Map 13
Germany, Upper, 193, 194; Map 13
Gerontia, Map 1
Gordium, Map 7
Gortyn(a), Maps 1, 6
Goths, 216
Gracchus, Gaius, 150
Gracchus, Tiberius, 149–50
Granicus, 97; Map 7
Gythium, Map 1

H

Hadria, Map 14
Hadrian, 194–5
Hadrian's Wall, 195; *178*, *193*; Map 13

233

Haliacmon, Map 1
Halicarnassus, Maps 1, 2, 6
Halonnesos, Map 1
Halys, 54
Hamilcar Barca, 132
Hannibal, 133–4
Hasdrubal, 133–4
Hebrus, Map 1
Helena, Map 1
Helice, Map 1
Helicon, Mt., *1*; Map 1
'Helladic' culture, 14–16
Hellenic League, 97
Hellespont (*Hellespontus*), 65; 97; Map 1
Helots, 28, 69
Helvetii, 162; Map 11
Hemeroscopeum, Map 3
Hephaestus, Temple of (Athens), *67*
Hera, 25
Heraclea, 130
Heracleitus, 54
Herculaneum, *115*
Hermes of Praxiteles, 100
Hermione, Map 1
Hermunduri, Map 13
Hermus, Maps 1, 2
Herodotus, 81–2
Herod the Great, 180
Hesiod, 43
Hestia, 44
Hestiaeotis, Map 1
Hibernia, Map 13
Hiberus, Maps 10, 13
Hieron I (king of Syracuse), 69, 98, 114
Hieron II (king of Syracuse), 131; *144*
Hierosolyma, Map 13; see JERUSALEM
Himera, 69; Maps 9, 14
Hippias, 42, 65
Hippocrates, 87
Hispania, Map 14
Histria, Map 14
Hittite empire, 25
Homer, 25, 26
Homeric Hymns, 43
Honorius, *222*
Horace, 178
'House of the Masks' (Delos), *202*
Huns, 216
Hydaspes, Map 7
Hydrea, Map 1

I

Ialysus, Maps 1, 2
Iaxartes, Map 7
Iazyges, Map 13
Iberia, Map 13
Icaria, Map 1
Iceni, 184
Icos, Map 1
Ictinus, 81
Ida, Mt., Map 1
Ilerda, 163; Map 11
Iliad, 25, 26, 43
Ilipa, 134; Map 10
Illyricum, Maps 9, 10, 12, 13
Ilva, Maps 9, 10, 14
Imbros, Maps 1, 2, 6
imperium, 116, 132, 168
India, 98, 103; Map 7
Indus, Maps 7, 8
Iolcos, 16
Ionia, Greek cities in, 56, 65, 67–8, 85, 97, 98
Ionians, 26; Map 2
Ios, Map 1
Irrhesia, Map 1
Isaeus, 99
Isara, Map 14
Isca, Map 13
Isis, 104, 210
Isocrates, 99
Issa, Map 9
Issus, 97; Map 7
Ister, 56; Map 7
Istrus, Map 3
Itanus, Map 1
Ithaca, Maps 1, 6
ius gentium, 149

J

Jerusalem (*Hierosolyma*), 55 (Fig.), 184, 195
Jews, 195, 196, 197
Josephus, 209
Judaea, 180; Maps 12, 13
Jugurtha, 151
Julian, 215
Jupiter, 116
Justinian I, 216; *224*
Juvenal, 200

L

Lacinium, Map 14
Laconi(c)a, 85; Maps 1, 2, 6

Laconicus, Sinus, Map 1
Lade, 56
Lampsacus, Map 6
Langobardi, Map 13
Laris(s)a, (Thessaly), Maps 1, 2, 6
Larius, Lacus, Map 14
Lars Porsenna, 114
latifundia, 136–7
'Latin colonies', 129, 150
Latin language, 216, 225
Latin League, 119, 120, 129
Latins, 12, 113, 116, 119, 120, 150; Map 9
Latium, 16, 113–16, 119; Map 14
Laurium, Mt., 11
law, Roman, 148–9, 214–5, 225
Lebedus, Map 1
Lemnos, Maps 1, 2, 6
Leo I, Pope, 216
Leonidas, 66
Lepidus, 161, 164; *153*
Lepsia, Map 1
Leptis Magna, *232*; Map 13
Leros, Map 1
Lesbos, 68 (Fig.), 84; Maps 1, 2, 6
Leuca, Mt., Map 1
Leucas, 68 (Fig.); Maps 1, 2, 6
Leuce Acte Pr., Map 1
Leucippus, 82
Leuctra, 85
Libya (Libyans), 13; Map 13
Licinius, 212
Liguria, Map 14
Ligurians, 135
Ligusticus, Sinus, Map 14
Lilybaeum, 132; Maps 10, 11, 14
limes, 214 (Fig.)
Lindum, Map 13
Lindus, *88*; Maps 1, 2
Linear A script, 14
Linear B script, 15 (Fig.), 16
Lion Gate (Mycenae), 15; *27*, *30*
Liparaeae I, Map 14
Lissus, Map 10
literature, Latin, 146–7, 167, 200–1, 214
Livius Andronicus, 146
Livy, 178

Locri Epizephyrii, Map 9
Locris, Maps 1, 2, 6
Locris Oz(olae), Map 1
Londinium, Map 13
Long Walls (Athens), 83
Luca, 163; Map 14
Lucan, 200
Lucania, Map 14
Lucanians, 129
Lucian, 209
Lucretius, 167
Lucullus, 162
Lugdunensis (Gaul), 180,
  184; Maps 12, 13
Lugdunum, Map 14
Luna, Map 14
Lusitania (Spain), 180, 184;
  Maps 12, 13
Lusitanians, 135; Map 11
Lutetia, Map 13
Lybia, 55 (Fig.)
Lycia, 182; Maps 8, 11, 13
Lydia, 29, 30, 54, 55, 68
  (Fig.); Maps 1, 2, 4, 5, 6
Lysias, 99
Lysippus, 100

M

Macedon(ia), 55 (Fig.), 65,
  68 (Fig.), 87–8, 97–8, 101,
  102, 134–5; Maps 1, 4, 5,
  6, 7, 8, 12
Macedonia (Rom. province),
  135
Macestus ,1
Maeander, Map 1
Magna Graecia, 27, 68–9,
  98, 114–15; 12
Magnesia ad Maeandrum,
  Map 6
Magnesia ad Sipylum, 134;
  Maps 1, 6
Malaca, Map 10
Malea Pr., Map 1
Mantinea, 85; 96; Map 1
Mantua, Map 14
Marathon, 65; 3, 50; Map 3
Marcellus, 179, 181
Marcomanni, 180, 196; Map
  13
Marius, 150–2
Mars, 130
Marsi, Map 9
Martial, 200
Massilia, 27, 150; Maps 3,
  10, 13, 14

Mauretania, 182; Map 12
Mausoleum of Halicarnassus,
  88, 100
Mausolus, 88
Maxentius, 211
Maximian, 211
Maximinus, 212
Medes, 54
Media, Map 7
Mediolanum, Map 13
Mediterranean (*Mare Inter-
  num*), 9–13, 130, 135;
  Maps 10, 13, 14
Megalopolis, Map 1
Megara, 31, 69, 70; Maps 1,
  2, 6
Megaris, Maps 1, 6
Melas, Sinus, Map 1
Melita, Map 10
Melos, 84; Maps 1, 2, 6
Memphis, 55 (Fig.); Maps
  7, 13
Menander, 103
Mende, Map 1
Mesopotamia, 194, 195;
  Maps 7, 8, 13
Messana (*Gr.* Messene),
  131; Maps 9, 10, 14
Messene (Peloponnesus),
  Map 1
Messene (Sicily), 69; see
  MESSANA
Messenia, 28, 69, 85, 86
  (Fig.); Maps 1, 2
Metapontum, Map 9
Metaurus, 134; Map 10
Methone, Maps 1, 6
Methymna, Map 1
metoikoi, 42
Miletus, 56; Maps 1, 2, 6
Milo, 163
Milvian Bridge, 211
Minoan civilisation, 13–14;
  13–24
Minos, 13
Misenum, Cape, *195*; Map
  14
Mithraism, 210, 215
Mithridates, 152, 162
Mitylene, Map 2
Moesia, 180, 193; Maps 12,
  13
Moguntiacum, Map 13
Monoecus, Map 14
mosaics, Roman, *169–171*,
  200–1, 205, 207

Mother Goddess, 14, 148
Motya, Map 9
Munda, 163; Map 11
Mutina, 135
Mycale, 67
Mycale, Mt., Map 1
Mycenae, 14–16, 25, 26; *25,
  27–31*; Map 2
Mycenaean civilisation, 14–
  16; *25–31*
Myconos, Map 1
Mylae, 132; Maps 9, 10
Myrtoum, Mare, Map 1
Mysia, 55 (Fig.), 68 (Fig.);
  Maps 1, 2, 6
Mysteries, Eleusinian, 53
Mystery cults, Eastern, 167,
  210 ,225
Mytilene, Map 1

N

Naevius, 146
Naples (*Neapolis*), 12; Maps
  9, 10, 13, 14
Narbo, 150; Maps 10, 13, 14
Narbonensis (Gaul), 151,
  180; Maps 12, 13
Narnia, Map 14
Naucratis, 27; Map 3
Naupactus, Map 6
Nauplia, Map 1
Naxos, 69, 70; Maps 1, 2, 4,
  6
Naxus, Map 9
Nemausus, Map 14
Nemea, Map 1
Neoplatonism, 210
Nero, 182–4
Nerva, 194
Nestus, Map 1
Nicaea (Bithynia), Council
  of, 215
Nicaea (Liguria), Maps 3,
  14
Nicias, 84
Nicias, Peace of, 84
Nicomedia, 212; Map 13
Nilus, Map 13
Nîmes, temple at, *160*
Nisyros, Map 1
Nora, Map 14
Noricum, 180, 216; Maps
  12, 13
Numantia, 135; Map 10
Numidia, 151; Maps 10, 11
Nura, Map 14

O

Ocha, Mt., Map 1
Octavian, 164–5, 167–8; see AUGUSTUS
Odessus, Map 3
Odoacer, 216
Odyssey, 26, 43
Oescus, Map 13
Oenussae I., Map 1
Oeta Mt., Map 1
Oetylus, Map 1
Olbia, Maps 3, 10, 14
Olympia, 28, 43, 68 (Fig.); *74*; Maps 1, 2, 6
Olympic Games, 28; *72, 73*
Olympus, Mt., (Lesbos), Map 1
Olympus, Mt. (Thessaly), Map 1
Olynthus, Maps 3, 6
Opis, 98; Map 7
Optimates, 162, 164
Orange, triumphal arch at, *148–9*
Orchomenus, Map 1
Orders, architectural, 44; *46–9, 107*
Ordymnus, Mt., Map 1
Orpheus, 53
Ossa, Mt., Map 1
Ostia, 119; *203–6*; Maps 10, 14
Otho, 184
Othrys, Mt., Map 1
Ovid, 178
Oxus, Map 7
Oxyrhynchus, Map 13

P

Pachynum Pr., Map 14
Padus, Maps 9, 10, 13, 14
Paestum, *12, 95*; Maps 9, 14
Pagasaeus, Sinus, Map 1
Palatine hill, 115, 197 (Fig.); *131, 172, 187*
Palestine, 184
Pallene, Map 1
Palma, Map 14
Palmyra, 211; *176*; Map 13
Pamphylia, Map 13
Panathenaic Festival, 41, 81
Pangaeus, Mt., 11, 88
Pannonia, 180; Map 12
Panormus, Maps 9, 10, 14
Panticapaeum, Map 3

Paphlagonia, Map 8
Papinian, 214
Parium, Map 1
Parma, 135; Map 14
Parmenides, 54
Parnassus, Mt., Map 1
Parnes, Mt., Map 1
Parnon, Mt., Map 1
Paros, Maps 1, 2, 6
Parthenon, 71 (Fig.), 81; *11, 58, 60–1*
Parthia (*Parthyaea*), 162, 163, 164, 179–80, 194, 195, 196, 211; Maps 7, 8
Parthorum, Regnum, Map 13
Patavium, Map 14
Patmos, Map 1
Patrae, Map 1
Paulus, 214
Paxos, Map 1
Peisistratus, 41–2
Pelion, Mt., Map 1
Pella, 68 (Fig.); Maps 6, 7, 8
Peloponnese (*Peloponnesus*), 28–9, 67, 85, 102; Maps 1, 4, 5
Peloponnesian League, 29, 85
Peloponnesian War, 83–5
penestae, 27
Peneus, Maps 1, 2
'Peoples of the Seas,' 25
Peparethos, Map 1
Pergamum, 101, 103, 135; *116–18, 234*; Maps 1, 6, 8, 13
Pericles, 70–2, 83–4
perioikoi, 28
Perrhaebi, Map 1
Persepolis, 55 (Fig.), 97; Maps 7, 8
Perseus, king of Macedon, 135
Persian Empire, 54–5, 67, 97, 98
Persian Gulf (*Sinus Persicus*), 54, 55 (Fig.)
Persians, 54–6, 65–8, 97
Persian Wars, 54–6, 65–8
Persis, 55 (Fig.); Maps 7, 8
Pescennius Niger, 210
Petra, 194; Map 13
Petronius, 200
Phaestus, *23–4*; Map 1
Pharae, Map 1
Pharsalus, 163; Maps 1, 11

Pharus, Map 9
Pheidias, 71, 81
Pherae, Map 1
Phigalia, Map 1
Philip II, king of Macedon, 87–8, 97
Philip V (king of Macedon), 134
Philip (Roman Emperor), 211
Philippi, 88, 164; Maps 12, 13
philosophy, Greek, 53–4, 99–100
philosophy, Roman, 209
Phlius, Map 1
Phocaea, Maps 1, 2, 6
Phocis, 28, 70; Maps 1, 2, 6
Phoenicians, 26, 130
Pholegandros, Map 1
Phrygia, 68 (Fig.); Maps 1, 2, 6
Phthiotis, Map 1
Picentes, Map 9
Picenum, Map 14
Picts, 216
Pindar, 69
Piraeus, 83; Maps 1, 6
Pisae, Maps 10, 14
Piso, 183
Placentia, Map 14
Plataea (*Plataeae*), 65; Maps 1, 4, 5
Plato, 99
Plautus, 147
Pliny the Elder, 200
Pliny the Younger, 209
Plotinus, 209
Plutarch, 209
Pola, Map 14
polis, 11
Polyaegos, Map 1
Polybius, 146
Polycleitus, 81
Polycrates, 55
Polygnotus, 81
Pompeii, 166; *208*
Pompey, 152, 161–3; *186*
Pont du Gard aqueduct, *167*
Pontus, 152, 162; Maps 8, 12, 13
Populonia, Map 14
'Porta Nigra' (Trier), *230*
portraiture, Roman, 167; *151–7, 159*
Portus Adurni, *190*

236

Poseidon, 25
Posidonia, Map 9; see PAES-
    TUM
Potidaea, 83, 84, 88; Maps
    1, 6
pottery, Greek, 43–4; *37–9,
    69–71, 100*
Praesus, Map 1
Praetorian Guard, 177, 181,
    182, 184, 213
Prasiae, Map 1
Praxiteles, 100
Priene, Maps 1, 2, 6
Princeps Civitatis, 168, 181
Principate, 167–84, 193–210
Proconnesos, Map 1
Propontis, 27, 70; Map 1
Propylaea, 71
Protagoras, 83
Provincia, Maps 11, 14
Ptolemaïs, Map 8
Ptolemies, 100, 101, 102,
    103
Ptolemy I (king of Egypt),
    101, 102, 103; *110–111*
Ptolemy (the geographer),
    209
publicani, 136, 165
Punic Wars, 130–5
Pydna, 88, 135; Map 1
Pylos, 15, 16, 25, 84; Map 1
Pyrrhus, 129–30
Pythagoras, 53, 54
Pytheas of Marseilles, 103

Q

Qalat Sem'an, 226
Quadi, 196; Map 13

R

Raetia, 180, 216; Maps 12,
    13
Ravenna, Maps 13, 14
Red Sea, 103
Regillus, Lake, 119
Regulus, 132
religion, Greek, 44–5
religion, Roman, 148, 177–
    178, 210, 215
Rhandeia, 183
Rhea Silvia, *130*
Rhegium, 69; Maps 9, 14
Rhenea, Map 1
Rhine   (*Rhenus*)   (Rhine
    frontier), 180, 181, 193,

195, 211; Maps 10–13
Rhodae, Map 14
Rhodanus, Maps 10, 14
Rhodes (*Rhodos*), 86 (Fig.);
    Maps 1, 2, 5, 6, 11
Rhyndacus, Map 1
roads, Roman, 129, 198;
    Map 14 (inset)
Roma (goddess), 178; *119,
    164*
Romulus, 115, *129*
Romulus Augustulus, 216
Royal Road, 55
Rubicon (*Rubico*), 163; Map
    11
Rusaddir, Map 10

S

Sabines, 129
Sabini, Map 14
Sacra, Via, *177*
Sagartii, 55 (Fig.)
Saguntum, 133; *143*; Map
    10
Salamis, 66–7; *52*; Maps 1,
    2, 5, 6
Sallentinum Pr., Map 14
Sallust, 167
Salonae, Map 13
Same, Map 1
Samnites, 120; Map 9
Samos, 55, 70, 86 (Fig.);
    Maps 1, 2, 4, 6
Samothrace, Map 1
Sant' Apollinare in Classe,
    225
Sappho, 43
Sardes, 55; Maps 1, 4, 5, 6, 7
Sardinia, 131, 132, 135;
    Maps 10, 12, 13, 14
Sarmatia, Map 13
Sarmizegetusa, Map 13
Saronicus, Sinus, Map 1
Sassanids, 211
Savus, Map 10
Saxons, 211, 216
Scamander, Map 1
Scandia, Map 13
Sciathos, Map 1
Scipio, Publius Cornelius,
    134, 146
Scipio Aemilianus, 146
Scopas, 100; *101*
Scots, 216
Scyros, Maps 1, 2, 6
sculpture, Greek, 81, 100,

103; *42–4, 63, 97–9, 101–2*
Segesta, Map 9
Segovia, aqueduct at, *228*
Sejanus, 181–2
Seleucia, 101
Seleucids, 100, 101, 102
Seleucus I (king of Syria),
    101; *109*
Selinus, Map 14
Seneca, 183, 200
Seriphos, Map 1
Sertorius, 161
Sestos, Map 6
Severus, Alexander, 210–11
Severus, Septimius, 210; *181*
Severus, Arch of, *187*
Sicani, Map 9
Sicily (*Sicilia*), 28, 68–9, 98–
    99, 131, 187, 135, 136;
    Maps 10, 12, 13, 14
Sicinos, Map 1
Siculi, Map 9
Siculum, Mare, Map 14
Sicyon, 31
Side, Map 7
Sidon, 55 (Fig.)
Sigeum, Map 1
Sila, Mt., Map 14
Silchester, *192*
Silures, 193
Singiticus, Sinus, Map 1
Sinope, Maps 3, 13
Siphnos, Map 1
Sirmium, Map 13
Siscia, Map 13
Sithonia, Map 1
slavery, Greek, 72
slavery, Roman, 166, 199
Smyrna, Maps 1, 2
Social War, 152
Socrates, 86
Sogdiana, 55 (Fig.), 98;
    Map 7
Solon, 32, 41–2, 43
Soluntum, Map 9
Solus, Map 9; see SOLUNTUM
Sophists, 86, 97, 99, 208
Sophocles, 82
Spain (*Hispania*), 131, 132–
    133, 135, 163, 180, 184,
    211, 216; Map 10
Spain, Further (Rom. prov-
    ince), 135
Spain, Nearer (Rom. prov-
    ince), 135
Sparta, 26–9, 66–7, 68
    (Fig.), 69–70, 83–5, 102;

90; Maps 1, 2, 4, 5, 6
Spartacus, 161
Spercheus, Map 1
Spina, Maps 9, 14
Sporades, Map 1
Stoa of Attalus, *68*
Stoicism, 101, 104, 148, 209
Strophades I., Map 1
Strymonicus, Sinus, Map 1
Suebi, 216
Suetonius, 209
Sugambri, Map 13
Sulla, 151–2, 161; *151*
Sulmo, Map 14
Sunium, Map 1
Susa (Italy), triumphal arch at, *168*
Susa (Persia), 55, 98; Maps 7, 8
Susiana, 55 (Fig.); Map 8
Sybaris, Map 9
Syracuse (*Syracusae*), 28, 68, 84, 98–9, 131, 132, 133; *89*; Maps 3, 10, 13, 14
Syria (kingdom), 100, 101, 102, 134; Maps 8, 11
Syria (Rom. province), 162, 193, 194, 211; Maps 12, 13
Syria Palestina, 195; see JUDAEA

T

Tacitus, 209
Taenarium Pr., Map 1
Tagus, Map 10
Tanagra, 70; Map 1
Tanagra statuettes, 33–4
Tanais, Maps 3, 7
Taras, Maps 3, 9; see TARENTUM
Tarentinus, Sinus, Map 14
Tarentum (*Gr.* Taras), 12, 129, 133; Maps 9, 10, 13
Tarquinii, Maps 9, 14
Tarquinius Priscus (king of Rome), 116
Tarquinius Superbus (king of Rome), 116
Tarraco, Maps 10, 13
Tarraconensis (Spain), 180; Map 13
Tarsus, Map 13
Taurasia, Map 10
Taxila, Map 7
Taygetus, Mt., Map 1

Tegea, 29; Map 1
Telamon, 132
Tempe, Vale of, 66; Map 1
Tempsa, Map 14
Tenedos, Map 1
Tenos, Map 1
Terence, 147
Tergeste, Map 14
Terracina, Map 14
Teutoburgian Forest, 181
Teutones, 151
Thales, 54
Thamugadi, Map 13
Thapsacus, 55 (Fig.)
Thapsus, 163; Map 11
Thasos, 11, 69; Maps 1, 4, 6
Thebes (*Thebae*) (Egypt), 55 (Fig.)
Thebes (*Thebae*) (Greece), 26, 67, 85, 88; *92*; Maps 1, 2, 6
Themistocles, 65–7
Theocritus, 103
Theodoric the Ostrogoth, mausoleum of at Ravenna, *223*
Theodosius I, 215
Theodosius II, 216
Theognis, 43
Theophrastus, 103
Thera, Maps 1, 2, 6
Therma, Map 5
Thermaicus, Sinus, Map 1
Thermopylae, 66, 134; *51*; Map 5
Theseus, 13, 31; *19*
Thesprotia, Map 1
Thessaliotis, Map 1
Thessalonica, Map 13
Thessaly (*Thessalia*), 15–16, 27, 66, 68 (Fig.), 69, 86, 134, 163; Maps 1, 2, 4, 6
Thrace (*Thracia*), 53, 55 (Fig.), 56, 68 (Fig.), 88, 180; (Rom. province), 182; Maps 1, 4, 5, 6, 13
Thucydides, 87
Thurii, 70, 129; Map 14
Tiber (*Tiberis*), 114, 115; Maps 9, 10, 14
Tiberius, 180, 181–2
Tibur, Map 14
Ticinus, Map 14
Tigranes, 162
Tigris, Maps 8, 13
Timgad, *194*
Timoleon, 99

Tingis, Maps 10, 13
Tingitana, Map 13
Tiryns, 15; *26*
Titus, 184, 193
Titus, Arch of (Rome), *172*
Tivoli, Villa of Hadrian at, *177*
'Tomb of the Leopards' (Tarquinii), *127*
Tomi, Map 13
Toronaicus, Sinus, Map 1
Torone, Map 1
Tragia, Map 1
Tragurium, Map 9
Trajan, 194
Trajan, Arch of (Benevento), *173*, *219*
Trajan, Basilica of (Rome), 199 (Fig.)
Transpadana, Map 14
Trapezus, Maps 3, 13
Trasimene, Lake, 133; Maps 10, 14
Trebia, 133
Tribonian, 215
Tripolis, Map 13
Triumvirate, First, 162
Triumvirate, Second, 164
Troas, Map 1
Troy (*Troia*), 25; Map 2
Truentum, Map 14
Tusculum, Map 9
Twelve Tables, Laws of the, 118, 146, 148
Tyras, Map 3
Tyre (*Tyrus*), 55 (Fig.), 97, 130; *114*; Maps 7, 13
Tyrrhenum, Mare, Maps 9, 14

U

Ulpian, 214
Umbria, Map 14
Umbrians (*Umbri*), Map 9
Utica, Map 10

V

Valens, 215
Valentia, Map 14
Valentinian, 215
Valeria, Via, *140*
Valerian, 211
Vandals, 216
Varus, 180

Veii, 120; Maps 9, 14
Velia, Maps 9, 14
Venetia, Map 14
Vercellae, 151
Verona, Map 14
Verus, Lucius, 195
Vespasian, 184, 193
Vesta, 148
Victory (Nike) of Samothrace, 103
Victory (Nike), Temple of (Athens), 71 (Fig.); 65
'Villanovan culture', 119
Viminacium, Map 13
Vindex, 184

Virgil, 178
Viriathus, 135
Vitellius, 184
Vitruvius, 209
Volaterrae, Map 14
Volsci, 119, 120; Map 9
Volsinii, Map 9
Volubilis, 197–8; Map 13
Vulci, Map 9

X

Xenophanes, 54
Xenophon, 85, 99
Xerxes, 65–7

Z

Zacynthos, 68 (Fig.); Maps 1, 2, 6
Zama, 134; Maps 10, 13
Zancle, Map 9; see MESSANA
Zela, Map 11
Zeno of Citium, 101, 104
Zeno of Elea, 83
Zenobia, 211
Zeus, 25
Zeus, Altar of (Pergamum), 103; 116
'Zeus of Olympia', 81; 44

Printed in the Netherlands